BLACKWEL
Oxford, Engl

In appreciation of
your kindness
and best wishes

Oxford 12, 9, 5 —

Charles Carr

THE PROBLEM OF POWER

THE PROBLEM OF POWER

POWER

The Reith Memorial Lectures
1951

By
THE RIGHT HONOURABLE
LORD RADCLIFFE OF WERNETH
G.B.E.

London
SECKER AND WARBURG
1952

MARTIN SECKER & WARBURG, LTD.
7, John Street, Bloomsbury,
London, W.C.1

First published 1952

Made and printed in Great Britain by
William Clowes and Sons, Limited, London and Beccles

ACKNOWLEDGEMENT

The Lectures in this volume were originally commissioned by, and delivered for, THE BRITISH BROADCASTING CORPORATION, by whose permission they are now printed in book form

CONTENTS

CONTENTS

LECTURE VI

LECTURE VII

FOREWORD

IT is not usual for an author to introduce his own work. I am doing so in this case only because I am taken aback at the thought that these radio talks should now take the solemn form of publication in a book. I do not think them suitable for that purpose and I should myself have been content that they should drift away on the air to which they were first committed. But my friends and publishers, Messrs. Martin Secker and Warburg, thought otherwise, though it is fair to them to say that they formed their resolution before they saw any of the scripts, and I hope therefore that nothing that I am now saying will injure the prospects of what they have so courageously undertaken. Accepting, then, that there is to be a book, I wish to enter one or two disclaimers for the benefit of those who may go on to read it.

The first relates to the form of these seven lectures. I am quite sure that I should not write in this way if I were writing deliberately for print. I have never yet written a book, so my literary style remains a question of hypothesis, but I have a strong personal conviction that it would not come out as these talks have come out. No one can prevent me thinking that it would have more balance, it would risk more complicated constructions, it would tend to be more musical, it would certainly have a greater content of allusion. These are all qualities that I admire in prose : and, since it has been my endeavour to eliminate them as far as possible from the script of my talks, I will defend myself briefly by explaining why I have been so austere in self-denial.

The preparation of the Reith Lectures for the B.B.C. has been to me a fascinating experience. Quite apart from the problem of what to say, there is the problem of how to say it. That problem is present, of course, in all broadcast speech. But it becomes more insistent in the case of the annual Reith Lectures, because they are given an importance that elevates them into one of the radio events of the year, because the expected length of each 'lecture—thirty minutes—is inordinately long for the attention of one's hearers, and, lastly, because they are a series to which the lecturer is doomed to return each Sunday for a period of weeks. Their mere recurrence imposes upon him a special form of self-consciousness which I myself have not been aware of when on other occasions I have been preparing scripts for single talks.

It is too portentuous to speak of new art forms, but what is the right form for this delivery, which is neither a conversation nor a speech nor a lecture nor a discourse? For, however much it may resemble some of these, it lacks the essential element of an audience that one can to some extent measure and respond to. Certainly I can find no useful analogue in conversation. It is quite a few years now since I first gave a broadcast talk and I think that there still lingered on at that time in the B.B.C. the old tradition that you delivered your talk on the assumption that you were addressing a friend seated in a chair on the other side of the table in the studio. I can only say that I have never had a friend who sat in a chair allowing me to address him uninterruptedly for as much as sixty seconds, and I am quite sure that any friend who expected a similar service of me would have put an end to our friendship long ago. Nor do my friends wish me to answer for them their own unspoken questions. On the contrary, they wish to fill the unforgiving minute with forty seconds of their own views. The fact is that a broadcast talk is not at all like a conversation, though there may be an art to make it seem so which a very few men possess: President Roosevelt and the late Mr. Middleton, for example. It is not like it, I would say, not merely because the talk is a monologue, but because

the casual enlargement of ideas, one of the essences of conversation, becomes impossible when there is no exchange of
speakers. A broadcast talk which really directed itself to
answering the imagined questions of imagined interlocutors
(I hope that this is not heresy) would be intolerably weak in
effect. Since the speaker is alone he must follow his own mind
or his own whim, in the hope that at least he can hang together what he says on the string of his own personality.
Otherwise he is not talking: he is merely replying.

Besides, conversation cannot take place with an individual
one knows as slightly as the listener on the Home Service
Programme. One can speak usefully, courteously, even
interestingly, with people one does not know: but to con-
verse with someone you must have a well-understood background of reference and allusion. If you have not, conversation becomes as tedious as the debates of an international
committee. Conversation is largely the creation of a coterie
and to those who do not belong to the coterie it is probably as
boring and artificial as any other esoteric art form. For the
members of the coterie, on the other hand, it is a very
enjoyable and, after all, a very harmless pleasure. Since I
could not claim to have ever belonged to a coterie, except
perhaps for a year or two in my Oxford days and just afterwards, I can speak of this without anticipation and without
regret: though I note that, if nowadays I cross the path of
some member of the old coterie out hunting on his own, we
still gesture to each other in the old sign language before we
part.

Fundamentally a broadcast talk is a discourse. If listening
to sermons played as large a part in our usual avocations as
they did in, say, the seventeenth and eighteenth centuries,
we should have, I think, a reasonable model upon which to
construct such talks. They would not be expected to be cosy,
they would not be expected to be matey. They would not
be whimsical nor would they be arch. I do not know why it

is so difficult to avoid archness when one is writing for the radio. It is something to do with the selfconsciousness that isolation develops and the uneasy knowledge that you will never be able to make a joke because you will not smile and you will not hear any of your listeners laugh. It is akin to the dilemma of the schoolmaster, whose jokes are always laughed at, but for many other reasons than because they are thought to be funny. Again and again I detected and eliminated notes of archness in my scripts: but all the same I am afraid that some remain. But there would be little temptation to that if one could imagine one's hearers as trained, let me say, by the sermons of John Donne. One could then give the discourse its proper value: one could be copious, tremendous, eloquent, allusive and serious. In fact one would have an art form ready for the purpose. Whether anyone would listen, I do not know. I suppose that reading Donne's sermons aloud is mainly a matter for the Third Programme: but supposing that there was a real live Donne and he was allowed to deliver his discourse in the Home Programme? Again I do not know. Anyway I am not he.

The task has been one of converting the written language that we all write, more or less, into the spoken language that we all speak, more or less. I have found this very difficult, but interesting. Anyone who is a trained speaker and who knows what he wants to say can speak without preparing the form of his speech: what comes out is speech, though it is frequently not grammar. I have sometimes been appalled when I have read the shorthand record of a speech I have made in a Law Court: it has seemed intelligible and adequate at the time, but in review only about one sentence in two is grammatically constructed and the sense is often obscure. But, as speech, it conveyed its meaning and was understood. The man who hammers out in advance a broadcast script has not this resource: he has got to write every word down, measure it and time it. Consequently it is very easy to slip back into the written language that he is trying to escape from.

Now my mentors in the B.B.C., to whose patience and skilled experience I owe much, without having always taken their advice, were insistent that scripts should avoid "literary" language. I am sure that that is sound advice, but I doubt if the English tongue allows it to be realised completely. I think that educated speech does normally carry a strong literary flavour. Surely it takes much of its colour and effect from doing so: for our literary traditions are so rich and so abundant, common literary associations have been so much a part of the daily life of educated people, that one can use the phrases and forms of literary language in ordinary speech without any conscious impression of quotation. For that matter quotation itself has more than one use in such speech. To eliminate these materials completely is to run the risk of flatness, a great danger for the broadcast lecturer. To retain them at all freely is, on the other hand, a technical disadvantage. Putting jargon apart, our written language does tend to produce concentrations of "heavy" words, especially when the subject is the abstract one of ideas. Often too these "heavy" words are of the same syllabic length. To a listener with only his ear to instruct him a sentence or two of this kind, unexceptionable in print, conveys no impression in speech, for the words fall dead on the ear. Incidentally, if any reader will trouble to read aloud this last sentence, he will see how unsuited it is for the spoken word. I am not quite clear why, but the microphone seems to be hostile to inversions of speech that would not be unnatural in writing. In fact, one often employs them in writing to achieve an emphasis that is not needed, I suppose, in speech. Speech employs the simpler order of arrangement and likes to run through its meaning without holding up the sense. This is hard for one whose education was based on the classical tongues, but I have spent a good deal of time in unwinding the sentences in my scripts, in striking out parentheses, and in breaking up any complicated grammatical constructions. I have also tried to unbalance where, in writing, I should have balanced, in the hope that by so doing I might relieve the tedium of what cannot but be a monologue, and I have from time to time deliberately concocted a straggling sentence in order to break the rhythm.

This concludes this tiresome confession, which is probably of interest only to the comparatively small band of future Reith lecturers. I do not think that I have succeeded in what I set out to do. Looking at these lectures, I am inclined to rank them neither as good literature nor as good speech. They are too self-conscious and mannered for the best form of speech, though I would be very interested to hear someone deal with the kind of subject that I have dealt with using only simple and natural language; and they have not even been allowed to try to become the best kind of writing. In fact, they have fallen between two stools; not from anxiety to sit on both but from reluctance to sit on either.

My second disclaimer relates to the subject of the talks. In this case I am not working up to an apology, for within their limits the talks have said more than I hoped to be able to say, which would be, I knew, much less than I think. But I do want a reader to be sure what their limits are. They are essays about an idea or, rather, about one or two ideas. They have no other connecting link than their relation to these ideas and, since the talks cannot usefully be altogether impersonal, their relation to my own views in the few places where those views are expressed. I think, myself, that some general understanding of these ideas is of very great importance to present and future society in this country. That is why I addressed myself to them when the B.B.C. did me the honour of inviting me to give the Reith Lectures for last year.

But I do mean, general understanding. The content of

these lectures is not worth the attention of those who have
already given their time and thought to the problems that I
have tried to touch upon. This is not a book for the expert,
and I am rather afraid that it will be of no practical use to the
student. I only hope that it will not actively mislead him. It
is less likely to do so if he appreciates from the start that the
three and a half hours' speaking time, which is the whole
extent of the talks, is not designed at all to contain a history
of thought on these topics (which I am not qualified to com-
pose and which has, anyway, been done by many others) or to
offer a summary of phases of thought about them (since I
have not even mentioned some of the greatest and most influential names). I have had to deal in some degree with
history, of which I am the merest amateur, because most
great books are written not about but against current conditions and some description of those conditions is therefore
necessary to do justice to the writer's real attitude. But I have
not written as a historian.

What I have tried to do is to interest my hearers in certain
ideas and to stimulate their curiosity as to the meaning and
value of what they have before, possibly, rather taken for
granted. My method has been to describe some great work,
some significant phase, of the past in order to let the present
be seen in relief. I have not tried to exhaust the questions
that I have raised or even to deal with them adequately:
much less have I tried to supply the answers. For one thing I
do not know the answers, since I think that the adventure of
human society is an endless one and that the " margin fades
for ever and for ever as we move". But in any event I do not
want to be a party to the idea that the function of broadcasting on the B.B.C. is to tell people what to think. I know
that there is the soft answer, "You can at any rate tell them
what *you* think"; nevertheless for most of us such a distinction is hard to draw and harder still to observe. Modern
methods of communication have made the expert so

unfortunately available to everyone that the power of independent thought is becoming atrophied, just as is the use of hands and legs. Perhaps we shall be losing a faculty that has brought with it as much malady as health: but for the time being I follow Pascal, "C'est donc la pensée qui fait l'être de l'homme, et sans quoi on ne peut le concevoir. . . . Travaillons donc à bien penser: Voilà le principe de la morale." We shall not think aright if we take our thinking in the form of predigested food. It is no good following authority unless you have some comprehension of what it stands for, and I do not think that that measure of comprehension is to be arrived at without the process of independent thought. So the aim of this book is not to inform or to instruct. Nor is it at all its aim to justify or to condemn any particular form of political society. If somebody would use the word "stimulating" about it I should be very content.

LECTURE I

LECTURE I

IF I speak of the Problem of Power, at least I do not mean that it is a problem whether power should exist or not. It is most inescapably present in modern society and its crowded civilisations. Such societies cannot be conducted at all without central authority to keep the whole activity from breaking down. And, just as to-day's social life requires the existence of power, so to-day's developments have furnished the means of that power becoming a strong force; even changes such as the greater ease and quickness of communication have worked to give it a sharp eye and a firm hand. Moreover, society has become used to the standing armies of power —the permanent civil service, the police force, the tax-gatherer—organised on a scale which was unknown to earlier centuries. So the philosophy of the backwoods is useless, because it is too simple, for the present age: the philosophy that goes to bed with the thought that the less authority men have over each other the better for all concerned, for then each man's native virtue will see him through.

The problem that I am thinking of is of a different order. It is the question, what really prevents men who have authority from abusing their authority? The other side of that problem is another question, what is it, if it is not force, that leads men to give obedience to authority? There is a certain amount of what I may call folk-lore to be cleared out of the way before one can begin to answer such questions. The people of these islands, who have shown in their history the most singular instances of great responsibilities worthily discharged, who have proved, one might say, most apt for power, have a wry native tradition that all men abuse

3

power and are the worse for having it. "All power tends to corrupt, and absolute power corrupts absolutely." Et cetera, et cetera. Like much folk-lore the legend is enjoyed but not necessarily believed. Since I do not myself believe it, for I think that most men are the better, not the worse, for having authority, I think that the legend is best attributed to that instinctive piety which leads men to denigrate what they dearly cherish. At any rate, I will not take the legend as a final answer to my question.

It is a problem that different societies may approach differently. But for this country it has to be seen against the background of European civilisation, for that civilisation and its ideas are part of the very structure of our political thinking. This is not an essay, then, in remaking society out of our own heads, but it does involve trying to see what really lies behind phrases such as "freedom", "liberty", "rule of law", which are, perhaps, so familiar, so automatic, that they have become more incantations than ideas. The ideas of democracy—to use another much-worn word—have suffered from democracy's own vast success, and as a result there has been a tendency to confuse its forms with its substance. Rousseau once said that States, like human bodies, begin to die from the moment of their birth and carry the causes of their own destruction within themselves. So it is with ideas. The ideas that the gods love die young before they have had time to grow tired. Perhaps no beliefs ever recover their own glad, confident morning: but it is possible for them to grow up while they change, so that by reinterpretation they may take on a new vitality. That is what makes it worth while to take one more glance at the familiar features of democratic society.

After all, what kills ideas is disillusion. And this is an age haunted by fear and disillusion; though that is not necessarily to our discredit. The disillusion comes to us by inheritance from the past and represents the accumulated disappointment of five centuries that the modern world which seemed to offer so much to the individual yet continues to withhold its best fruit from his grasp. Certainly it has brought him great benefits, but peace of spirit is not among them. If one assumes that our age began with the cult of the individual, critical, independent and self-reliant, it looks as if it may end with the virtual destruction of all true individuality. Indeed it is not easy to feel sure that the virtues which one was taught to admire—the heroic qualities, the overmastering vision, gallantry, chivalry—are not survivals from a different order of things for which society is coming to have no use. There would be much to fear in that alone. But there is other reason than that for fear. This is a generation that has seen the powers of evil menacingly at large. It is left without excuse for any failure to realise the existence of those powers or the magnitude of the challenge that every civilisation always has to face. The great forces that govern the world have made no covenant that particular ideas or particular forms of society shall always triumph or always endure, and one thing that a backward glance helps to recall is that men have lived their lives nobly, and wielded power nobly, too, under systems of ideas very different from those that rule in our society to-day.

That is my main reason for looking backwards in these lectures; to take up here some great book, to take up there some significant episode, and to see what sort of light they throw upon present problems. I am not tracing any history of ideas, because the historical development itself is not my concern—nor will I spend time in trying to discuss the merits of different kinds of societies—monarchies, aristocracies, democracies, mixed constitutions and what not. Such comparisons are rather sterile, on any view. And even if, at the end, the theorist were to say, for instance, that he preferred an aristocracy, with its diffused power, its sense of order, its endowed public service, the preference would be of no practical importance, because such things as aristocracies cannot be made by taking thought. They make themselves, in course of time and under special conditions : and they generally unmake themselves by the same process. So the society that I think of is a democratic society such as we now have in this country, however far it may be convenient to travel away from it, in hope of seeing its ideas more clearly on return. I dare say that it is fated to pass, is even now passing, into other forms; if you will, into the new managerial society, to use a current phrase. If so, it will have a new type of governors, selected in some new way. Actually, however generous the democratic theory, there is always, I think, something like a governing class, endowed, or privileged, or co-opted; for the great majority of men, demonstrably, do not want to take any active part in political life. But whatever may be the method by which men may come to authority over other men, the same problems will still remain for all but monsters : For what purpose? Under what limitations? With what sanctions? And, for better or for worse, the answers for this country must somehow be related to our own history and to the history of the civilisation of which it forms part. And so I turn to Plato.

It is the inevitable transition. Political theory as known to us did not begin with Plato, but once he had written his book *The Republic* in the fourth century before Christ, the political thought of the Western world could never afterwards be free from the influence of what he had said. That is some measure of his greatness. Again : take up any one of its ten books and start reading in it: once you have got accustomed to the maddening process of argument by logic and reminded yourself that he was writing for what must have been incomparably the finest-witted race the world has known, you will find that every few pages you have put the book down and begun to apply something that he has said to a piece of later history or to the current problems of our own world. That is because, while he was writing about what mattered immensely to him in the politics of fourth-century Greece, what he was trying to find an answer to were the fundamental questions: the purpose and destiny of the individual; and the purpose and justification of the State, that political instrument which is fashioned by individuals but shows often so little of their own image.

The Republic, the book that was to continue the model State, is a sad book. Plato's philosophical system is responsible, though at some removes, for the word Idealism, and those men who can let their minds dwell upon perfect forms without shutting their eyes to very imperfect reality are likely to be more great than gay—such was Plato. And he was writing in a period of disillusion. Within one man's lifetime Athens, his native State, had reached a height of glory— mistress of the surrounding seas, centre of a maritime and trading empire, liberal, wealthy, brilliant and cultivated— and then descended to a fallen and distracted city. A long war with her rival, Sparta, had exhausted Athenian power and, not for the last time in history, what was liberal and humane was seen to go down before the forces of all that was most puritan and narrow. Failure abroad had led to failure of spirit at home and a democracy, so recently united, self-confident and proud of its leaders, had turned to a rout of little men more anxious to blame others than to take responsibility upon themselves. Every liberal civilisation has to absorb an intake of self-criticism: but there seem to be in history certain special periods of disillusion, when everyone has suddenly become too sharp for loyalty, whether to old beliefs or to new truths. Criticism at such times is used not to test but to destroy values, and it wipes out all distinction between things that matter and things that do not. Scepticism of this kind was an outrage to Plato; and he set himself to uproot the crop of doctrines that grow out of it. They are still fairly familiar and so, I suppose, have an immortality of their own.

There is no such thing as justice in a state; it is merely a fiction that men, who are conscious of their individual weakness, think up to keep the wild men down. Or it is a word that the people in power use in order to give a moral cover to what is really their own material interest. Or again, as Nietzsche argued, the only thing that deserves to be called Justice is the will of the strong man: all else is "slave-morality".

Plato would have no truck with any of this. To him human life had no meaning unless its purpose was first to understand and then to pursue what was True and Good and Beautiful. I speak those words in capitals and then I leave them, leaving too the question unresolved how far they stand for anything that has a definite meaning. He at any rate thought that they had meaning enough to describe the true purpose of human life, and for him the question "What do men organise themselves into society for?" could have only one answer: "To give the members of society, all the members, the best chance of realising their best selves." So, in one leap, there is made the big decision: the State is an organisation which exists for a moral purpose, to make its citizens better men, indeed to see that they are better men, and unless it deliberately tries to reach this end, it might as well not exist. Whatever else it does, such a conception of the State makes the duty of those who are to hold power in it an elevated one.

How to find people good enough for this task of holding power? To answer, "Get the best men", is the answer of every amateur in politics: but it leaves every practical problem connected with it still unsolved. Plato did not ignore the practical problems, which he profoundly understood, but his solution is the outcome of his very individual approach. He was a passionate specialist. He could not stand the idea of a jack-of-all-trades, the man who can turn his hand to many things without mastery of any. Plato had what is threatening to become rare, a reverence for a craft; and he looked on statesmanship as the supreme craft to which, more than to any other, a man should be apprenticed by long training and to which his life must be dedicated. Inevitably therefore to him "rulers" must be somehow a class apart, a trained professional body, whom it would be out of the question to choose or to remove by the rough-and-ready methods of popular election. And, perhaps no less inevitably, he thought it an obvious proposition that, making all allowances for education and training, only some men are capable of exercising power. He had seen in Athens the practical application in politics of the famous dogma, All·men are by nature created equal, and it had seemed to him—well, I think that it had seemed to him like being flippant about serious matters. For, again, he was to a degree that we can hardly grasp, wholly an intellectualist. He did believe that human reason was the divine attribute of humanity, and that nothing that reason could not justify as valid could be right. Not for him the saving qualifications of more fuzzy minds— the "Well, you know, after all", kind of conclusion. I do not mean by that that Plato thought life explicable by a dry logic: on the contrary, reason to him was the trained exercise of man's highest qualities in combination and it included as much man's natural attraction to what he feels to be fine as his arguments to prove that it is fine. A man with such an attitude may be something of a Puritan—which Plato certainly was; but I do not think that he is likely to be a prig— which Plato most certainly was not.

So in his model State, the Republic, its members are to be divided into three classes : not according to social position or difference of wealth, but according to the kind of person that each is supposed to be. There is the ruling class, with absolute power, unfettered by law : they are to consist of persons capable of the highest range of reason and self control. Next to them, acting as a sort of Prætorian Guard, is the class of warriors, conspicuous in the qualities of courage and devotion, but a little below the best, we must assume, in the field of intellect. And below them come the rest, the great body of citizens, pursuing the ordinary callings of daily life and characterised by Plato, rather unfairly, as those whose lives are dominated by the third main element in the make-up of the human being: the desire for gain. These classes, once formed, are to be virtually static, a system of caste, from which there might be promotion or demotion only in a few exceptional cases. For Plato was one of the earliest believers in eugenics, and, since he also believed that women ought to be admitted to the highest class in common with men, he counted on maintaining its quality by a combination of selective breeding and rigorous education.

Now that was to be the Constitution of the Republic and it was to be nearly all the constitution that it was to have. It is a scheme which at first sight seems to challenge most accepted ideas of a healthy society, yet it is the scheme produced by the most elevated mind of the ancient world. The truth is that Plato cared so very much more about the result than any ordinary man will allow himself to do. He was ready to sacrifice so much to achieve the result. He had come to the conclusion—and I dare not call him old-fashioned or out of date—that it was useless to hope for a perfect society in which everyone should be treated honestly and fairly but according to his capacity, unless that society could be ruled by men who had been specially bred, trained and exercised for the task and then given uncontrolled authority to fulfil it. To him the problem never even presented itself as one of finding the proper limits to State power: his whole concern was to discover how to prevent even the best men abusing the absolute power that they must have.

Everything was to be required of then in exchange for this privilege of power. They were to have neither private property nor family of their own. Supported in the mere essentials by contributions from the other classes, living in

common and eating at a common table, they resemble some
strange college, half professors, half warrior knights. One
pauses a little horrified at this plan of a communism that was
to extend to wives as well as property. In the book of his old
age, *The Laws*, Plato himself receded from this as from some
other of his plans. But in putting it forward he had found a
provocative way of saying a true thing. Men do not abuse
power, in general, out of caprice or mad vanity or from a
tyrant's whim: they abuse it to hold on to or gain material
things, for themselves or their class, or to provide advantage
for their families. It is in that sense that power corrupts; and
since, thought Plato, no man is good enough to resist this
subtle, half-benevolent corruption, then away for good with
the causes of it. Those who would hold power must abjure the
temptations of human affection or material things. Material
wealth, or at any rate the faulty distribution of wealth, was to
him the source of most evils. Indeed, long before Disraeli had
spoken of the Two Nations—the rich and the poor—Plato
was writing the two cities, hostile to each other, that you will
find in any one city where wealth is not justly divided.

It is philosophers, then, who will rule in his State. No
real hope for the world until the day when philosophers
become kings or kings turn philosophers. For this almost a
lifelong education must be undertaken by those who are to be
fit for power. The purpose of the education is not to make
them masters of practical affairs but to give them what Plato
calls the "idea of good"—the ability to reason constructively
about general ideas and to arrive at a personal vision of the
unalterable values of truth and beauty—not merely, like
lesser men, to have opinions about them.

But would such men be willing to take the burden of power,
to spend their lives in looking after the welfare of other men?
Most people, I think, would answer "No." They would expect
men trained by such elevated studies—listed by Plato as
arithmetic, geometry, astronomy, harmonics and dialectic—

to shun the political arena in which men compete "not without dust and heat". All the moral dignity of *The Republic* is shown in its answer to this question. No man of developed mind, it is taken for granted, would want power: why should he? The philosopher in politics is "a man among wild beasts". Even if things so come about that he is found possessing power, there is no likelihood that its possession will bring him happiness. But that, says Plato, is not the point. It is just because this man does not want power, just because he does not look to it to bring any happiness or practical advantage to himself, that he, and only he, is fit to exercise it. And he will accept the burden that he has not sought as something which his duty binds him to—since he owes both his duty and his will to do it to the society that made him.

And so we have the unforgettable picture of the philosopher-ruler going down into the cave, leaving the clarity and serene light that is natural to his own mind for the dark half-world of those that he must serve. The cave is the home of those who do not have the vision to see things in the unsparing light, who see, as in a glass darkly, only the shadows and reflections of things as they really are. It is, in fact, the world of ordinary people: of confusion and muddle and half-truth. But it is also the place in which the affairs of ordinary people must be conducted, and so the place in which the statesman, however elevated his thought or clear his vision, must do his work—or theirs. There, in the half-darkness, as the shadows flicker and the very light deceives, the philosopher's pure vision is at first a disadvantage. He will peer and stumble, and the cave-dwellers will laugh at him and his tales of a sunlit world outside. But not for ever, Plato says— "Down you must go then, each in his turn, to the habitation of the others and accustom yourselves to the observation of the obscure things there. For once habituated you will discern them infinitely better than the dwellers there, and you will know what each of the images is and of what it is a

LECTURE II

LECTURE II

WHEN I spoke of Plato last week I described how he believed—or almost believed—in the possibility of a perfect human society and how, for the chance of creating this, he was prepared to see absolute and unrestrained power placed in the hands of a few special individuals. Now, if you turn to the Middle Ages, you perceive men's minds dominated by beliefs that are nearly the direct opposite of these. The period of the Middle Ages represents many centuries in time; but it was the character of medieval thought to see human society and man's life in society not so much as episodes distinct in themselves, with a meaning and significance of their own, but as part of the greater, eternal society whose destiny it was to fulfil God's purpose with the world. There might be justice in the world—certainly, there ought to be justice if only men would follow right reason and God's will—but the perfect society, as the perfect man, was something that could not in the nature of things be realised in a form of life whose values at the best were but transitory and provisional. Such a view, essentially religious, gave a peculiar status to the holder of power. On the one hand, it exalted political office. The ruler could be spoken of as God's direct representative on earth, his relation to the State a reflection of God's relation to the World: "The figure of God's majesty, His captain, steward, deputy elect." Political power in this setting carried the obligation of religious duty: "through this crown you become a sharer in our Ministry" were the words in which the Archbishop administered the Coronation oath to the King of France. Had not St. Paul himself said, in one of those fateful sentences that haunted

19

the medieval mind, "there is no power but of God: the powers that be are ordained of God. Whosoever therefore resisteth the power resisteth the ordinance of God: and they that resist shall receive to themselves damnation"? The holder of power, then, could claim that he was in some sense Priest as well as King.

But, on the other hand, this religious attitude was strong in its restraint of power; at any rate until, with the break up of the medieval system, monarchy was endowed with the theory of divine right, and what had been before acknowledgement of duty became instead a claim to privilege, thereby following what seems to be some fatal law of human affairs. For, in the true middle-age, absolute power would have been an impious as well as an impossible conception. It was impossible because the feudal system itself diffused power and made of the King less a sovereign than a chief among his barons, who in some countries actually elected him. It was impossible because physical conditions and the smallness of the economic scale impeded any supreme central power. But it was impious because men did genuinely believe that there was all the difference in the world, or all the difference in the next, between what you could do and what you ought to do in political life. For anyone dazed with the loud commands of modern life—"what public opinion requires", "the will of the people", "the declared will of Parliament"—to turn away to the political thought of the Middle Ages is to enter some quiet, magnificent cathedral from the noise and glare of the market place. "The King is under no man, but he is under God and the Law." That is Bracton speaking, an English lawyer of the thirteenth century. "It is beyond controversy among all good men that if the persons in authority command anything contrary to Natural Law or the Divine Precepts, it is not to be done." That is Grotius speaking, a Dutch lawyer of the sixteenth century. And both of them knew that they were saying nothing that had not been accepted doctrine in

Christendom for centuries : not only in England and Holland but in Spain and France and Italy and Germany. And they were speaking not of usurped authority or of powers to which no allegiance was due but of regular, duly constituted authority. And they were saying, in effect, that those who hold political power must adapt themselves to the moral order, if they want to claim obedience : that the moral order cannot be required to adapt itself to them.

Does it matter to us to-day that people talked and thought like this such a long time ago? As to that there are one or two things to be said. I am speaking in the briefest generalisations about a great period of time, something far longer than what we may call the Modern Age, during which portentous shapes of history formed and dissolved. Indeed you can start the Middle Ages and end them almost where you like, for they are part of one continuous process coming out of the antique world and the Dark Ages and shading into the world of to-day. Take it that the Middle Ages were at their flower in the thirteenth century: that their first beginnings lie with St. Augustine and the fall of Rome in the fifth century after Christ and their end somewhere between the fifteenth and seventeenth centuries: that covers a very long stretch of human experience. To me it makes it the more formidable that one can speak so generally of their thoughts and beliefs, that men did in so many countries and through so many generations think alike about the basis of political power. They did not live up to their principles, often they lived tragically below them. But history is as much the history of men's ideas as of their actions, which, once done, survive only as the expression of ideas. Besides, who can weigh the conduct of a whole epoch against its faiths, its failures and its penitence?

The real difficulty for those who are not scholars is to see the Middle Ages as a reality. The climate of belief has changed so much. To see them as a reality requires that we should take them on their merits. To do it needs, at first, an effort of mind and imagination. We live among visible relics of their civilisation: castle, common, abbey, cathedral and village church. But how to recreate the world in which those things were the centres on which life turned? To visualise a royal court in which jester and monarch each had his part; to see the Emperor of the world a bare-foot penitent at Canossa or our Henry II scourged kneeling before Becket's tomb at Canterbury? We may well wonder what sort of men they were, these men to whose eyes the crown and sceptre of earthly dominion must always figure the mocking reed and the crown of thorns. Their kind of world, their structure of ideas, has vanished, perhaps for ever, but out of what they believed, and argued about and in the end gave up believing have come the creeds—if that is the right word for them—that rule to-day.

The King then, all holders of political power, were under Law. One must try to give a meaning to that claim. It depends on certain suppositions. One is that there is a fixed order of the world valid for all peoples and at all times. But, if so, mankind is one community. A belief to which, despite every set-back, the world is now struggling to return. Generally Christendom was thought of as the world community, for, since God himself had founded it and had established the order which was to govern it, only the boldest spirits could include in the community peoples who did not acknowledge the Christian's God. But, within that conception, one God, one government, and so one Law.

That Law was a fixed set of principles which mere human beings had no power to tamper with. The idea of law-making —that is, imposing upon people as their rule for the future something that was to be a new rule or even a reversal of the existing rule—that idea was repugnant to the medieval idea of what Law meant. Of course, in this I am committing an enormous generalisation. Statutes and Ordinances were made

by kings' and by Parliaments: but more as a declaration what
the Law really was, what it had always been, than as a claim
that any persons, however great or wise or representative,
could have power to reverse or enlarge the set principles of
Law. Custom (which is, after all, a long-drawn-out process of
law-making by generations of people) and the eternal principles of conduct (the Law of Nature, as it was most generally
called) both set limits which no political power, representative
or non-representative, had the right to overstep. The
authority which ignored these limits, whatever they were, was
a tyrant, its orders were no orders and no obedience was due
to it or them.

I said its "limits, whatever they were", because so vast a
conception might well suggest that we were speaking of some
cloudy theory dreamed up by monks in their cells, and that
this Law, eternal and supreme, could never be more than an
abstraction, lacking concrete terms. Nor could it be much
more in an age of popular scepticism. But the medieval
doctors did not shrink from details. They were, it is true, men
of the schools, but many of them played a practical part in
state affairs. Indeed they were often the only persons
equipped to do so. Some of the best known names are found
conducting foreign missions for their country. They moved,
speaking a common diplomatic language, in a Europe that
was an international community: they could count upon
finding a common culture and institutions that had a strong
family resemblance to each other. I am not sure that Europe
has ever been closer since. This in itself gave raw material
from which the rules of the Law of Nature could be extracted:
whatever seemed to be the common practice of all civilised
or Christian peoples. Another source lay in the writings of
wise men of the past: for wherever they could be shown to
be in general agreement on some matter, it could be taken
that there lay authority itself. Then there was the body of
Roman Law, for the Romans, founders of the last great

universal order, had been faced with something of the same problem of finding the fundamental rule : the rule of "natural justice, equity and good conscience", as we used to instruct our own colonial administrators. And, more important than any of these, there were the Scriptures, in which God himself had spoken.

Over all this material brooded or played the medieval mind, learned, imaginative and credulous. In their way its possessors were intellectualists as ardent as the Greeks and they believed that whatever reason, Right Reason, could fairly deduce from these sources was universal truth. But they lacked a critical sense. Sometimes one does not know whether to smile or to tremble when one sees some great political consequence being deduced from a remote incident of the Old Testament or a phrase, taken out of its context, from the new. A monarch's claim to rule by divine commission turns out to have its source in the 13th verse of the 2nd chapter of 1st Epistle of Peter : in David's command to Abishai not to kill the sleeping Saul—"for who can stretch forth his hand against the Lord's anointed, and be guiltless?" —and in the passage from the Romans that I have already quoted. And the words "Compel them to come in" had a fatal influence in the history of religious persecution.

But, be that as it may, it was a thing as grand as this that Law meant to the medieval mind. It is worth a moment's pause to reflect how much less than this it means to-day, under a different system of ideas, and to ask whether, with all our gains, we have not, in this, lost something that was a powerful bond of civilisation, because it bound power itself. We cannot speak of Natural Law as these men did, for we hardly believe in its existence. It is "the unrevealed law of God", said Aquinas : to be revealed by the light of the intellect which, he held, was given by God. It was the "participation of the rational creature in the eternal law." Law was the "mind and will of God"; so taught the great school of civil lawyers at Bologna. It was "reason drawn from the mind of God and free from all changeableness": that was the definition of Mariana, a sixteenth-century Spaniard. It was above God himself, said Grotius, since not even He could change it. It was, to these men, the highest expression of human reason, divine in origin, and all human laws and ordinances must be in conformity with it or be nothing.

The idea itself is as old as man's conscience. Always there have been individuals ready to meet an obligation which they feel to be higher than any human authority and if conflict comes even to defy authority to the death. This sense of ultimate duty was a theme of the great Greek tragedians: it was the theme of much that was taught by the Hebrew prophets. Socrates, who was sent to his death by the people of Athens because he would not stop saying what they disliked to hear, closes his last speech with the words, "Athenians, I hold you in the highest regard and love: but I will obey God rather than you." But what is remarkable about the thought of the Middle Ages is that it made the idea of a supreme Law of Nature an idea that was commonly, even universally, accepted and it took the idea so seriously as to work out of it a regular system. Nor has it proved an idea that it has been easy to kill. When in time the medieval sense of community gave way before the rise of national states and Europe became a quarrelsome family of sovereign powers, international law had, as it were, to be invented in order to provide some structure upon which to build their relations with each other; and the Law of Nature is one of the founding fathers of international law. It is not spoken of now, in this country, as one of the elements of our own legal system. That is because men are broken in to looking to Parliament as the sole source of new or altered law and we take our existing law from a complicated network of past statutes, precedents and decided cases. But the Law of Nature is not so far behind us, after all. Here is Blackstone, eighteenth-century judge, whose *Commentaries* on the law of England are to-day not much more than old-fashioned. "This Law of Nature," he says, "being co-eval with mankind and dictated by God himself, is of course superior in obligation to any other. It is binding all over the globe, in all countries and at all times; no human laws are of any validity, if contrary to this; and such of them as are valid derive all their force and all their authority, mediately or intermediately from the original." I suspect Blackstone of quoting, rather automatically, some contemporary on the Continent, perhaps Burlamaqui or Montesquieu, and his idea of the Law of Nature is a much more pedestrian affair than that of the Middle Ages. In fact he tells us in one place that it comes down to the simple, though undistinguished, precept that man should pursue his own happiness. But, wakeful or sleepy, it is rather startling to find a judge almost in modern times advancing the proposition that all laws are over-ridden by these abstract principles.

If you tried to apply such a proposition, it would reduce to chaos and anarchy the modern highly organised State. Anarchy, of course, is a relative term. It is not one that unduly alarmed the men of the Middle Ages, who enjoyed, anyway, a fairly chaotic civil life. Strong centralised power was normally lacking, as it always will be when aristocracies flourish; and the apparatus of the modern State—regular army, police force, permanent administrative departments and great efficiency in tax-gathering—had not then been set up. There was some point therefore in asking whether one ought to obey a particular law or under what conditions laws were binding. It was not just a question of having to obey them or take the consequences.

The conception of a universal moral Law, ruling majestic-ally over human affairs, is a religious conception. But the medieval world is only intelligible as a world conceived in terms of religion. Because it was so conceived, the Holy

Roman Empire, little more than a dream as an achievement, remains still the perfect embodiment of the political thought of the Middle Ages. It was to have two heads, Pope and Emperor, who were to wield the two swords, one of spiritual, the other of temporal, power. It was to be a universal empire embracing the community of mankind. And it was to realise on earth the Kingdom of God. Its founder was Charlemagne, whose favourite book, we are told, was St. Augustine's *City of God*. What this empire might have become during the 1000 years of its nominal existence is one of the unanswered guesses of history: for even in the centuries when it had real and powerful existence it met shipwreck on the controversies between Pope and Emperor. Power is so greedy a thing that it cannot even share the world between two thrones. No one doubted that the Emperor held his temporal power of God: but did he hold it directly from God or indirectly, with the Pope between them, one step above him, as it were? The present day must leave to the antiquarian the details of that long controversy, though it produced some of the great political books of the Middle Ages. But I have found nothing that gives more pungently the peculiar flavour of the period than some of the claims that the Popes and their party made in asserting the supremacy of the cleric. "Priests," said Hincmar, "are the thrones of God, in whom He has his seat and through whom He declares His judgements." "The glory of Princes", said Ambrose, "is to the glory of Bishops as the brightness of lead to that of gold." And, lastly, "Priests have the greater authority," wrote Pope Gelasius, "since they will answer to the Lord even for Kings at the last judgement."

Perhaps one way of measuring how far the world has come from the Middle Ages would be this. Then conflict between Church and State was a dispute how far the Church could intervene on secular affairs because of their significance to religion; now it is a dispute how far the State can intervene on religious affairs because of their secular import.

Among the writings which contributed to form the thought of the Middle Ages, the works of St. Augustine stand apart. He was dead before the Middle Ages could be said to have been born, and he was too individual a genius to stand as any type of medieval doctor. Much that was claimed by the medieval Church would have been rejected by him. But the climate of thought, with its spiritual ambition, its other-worldliness, owes so much to his impulse that it seems vain to speak of it without saying something of him. In particular, of his book, or rather his twenty-two books, which bore the title *The City of God*. A proud, powerful and elo-quent book: discursive, long-winded and overweighted with dead theological controversies: but insisting again and again upon the message that was to stamp itself upon the mind of his successors—the institutions and the glories and the rewards of this world are nothing except as seen in the light of God's purpose through eternity. There are two cities or two societies that divide the world from the beginning to the end of time, the earthly society made up, as he says, of "all men who love pride and temporal power with vain elation and pomp of arrogance, and all rational spirits who set their affections on such things, and seek their own glory in the subjugation of man", and the heavenly society which has "truth for its king, love for its law, and eternity for its measure". These societies are divided because they have different wills or purposes, and the heavenly society, which embraces in one union the dead as well as the living, angels as well as men, heathen as well as Christians, is inspired by "the love of God in contempt of self".

This is not any definite political theory. Nor is it anything explicitly to do with the relations of Church and State. On the contrary, it is an attempt by a Christian bishop of the fifth century after Christ to express in words a profound vision of the meaning of man's life and its relation to the universe. But to reject the institutions of civil society—the magistrate, the tax-gatherer, property, slavery—as having no ultimate value in the light of eternity does nothing in itself to deny their actual existence, and Augustine faced the task of expounding to his Christian flock what measure they were to take of these institutions. The answer that he gave, though it is wholly ambiguous, was destined to have great influence upon the Western World.

One aspect that he dwells upon is that Christians are like pilgrims passing through this world. What concern have they with its temporal pomp? The royal procession goes by on its course and the pilgrim stands in the crowd of bystanders and takes off his hat, but it is nothing to him whether the king rules well or ill. "It is advantageous for all when good men rule," says Augustine, "but what matters it under what government a mortal man lives out his brief span? Evil rulers can do the good man no harm." Words that were to be echoed curiously by the English Wycliffe in the fourteenth century: "Servitude is of three kinds: as it denotes subjection to God, to man, and to sin; of these the first is excellent, the second is a matter of indifference, the last the worst possible." No wonder, then, that later centuries were to draw upon the immense authority of Augustine for the extremest doctrines of submission to the powers that be. And when Gibbon teased the early Christians with rejecting all the graces of society and Rousseau attacked them for rejecting society itself, it has to be admitted that they had plenty of material to found upon.

But this represents only one branch of Augustine's thought. More important, I think, is his main theme that, though the earthly society could not have justice in the true sense, for its dominant purpose was not to follow the way of God, yet it had justice "of a kind" which was good in its fashion. The State (and now he is thinking of actual States, not of an imaginary society) brought order and peace, both good things; and it protected institutions, such as property, which were needed in this world "to avoid worse". For man was by nature evil by reason of the Fall, and only a portion of mankind would ever be redeemed by the operation of Grace: therefore we should respect civil society as suited to the weakness of man's condition. This seems to me more acceptable a doctrine than the complete indifferentism of his other view. Indeed, Augustine was the last man to turn his back upon the manly virtues out of which great States are made. The Roman Empire itself, the very type of a city that was not of God, earns his praise, his admiration, I think, for the qualities of fortitude and devotion that had been shown in its history.

Augustine wrote his book at a time when Rome, the universal empire that for centuries had dominated the imagination of the civilised world, was falling. In 411 A.D. the capital itself was captured by the Goths. He meant to show by his book that God's purpose with the world did not depend on the rise or fall of earthly kingdoms. Whatever you make of the demonstration itself, there is no escape from the feeling that you are in the hands of a great tragic writer. Tragic, because he has the sense of the futility and yet of the beauty of human things. It was this sense, as I read his *Confessions*, that drove him from his first devotion to pagan philosophy to become a convert to Christianity. In many passages of *The City of God* he criticises the ethical systems of the ancient world. He sees them as a vain attempt by proud and shallow men to make for themselves a happiness in this vale of tears. He rejects them with the nervous anger of the convert. Augustine in fact never lost his early devotion to Plato, most spiritual of all philosophers (the title *The City of God* is itself taken from Plato's *Laws*), and he will not go to heaven without Plato in his company. One chapter of the 8th Book is, characteristically, headed "Whence Plato might have that knowledge that brought him so near the Christian doctrine."

Augustine was not one of those Christian apologists, of whom there have been too many, who seem to think that pagan ethics begin and end with the motto "Let us eat and drink to-day, for tomorrow we die." He keeps his most determined criticism for the Stoics, noblest Romans of them all, who held that virtue was its own obligation and that a man could die, if he could not live, with dignity. But, says Augustine, life measured in human terms is an inescapable disaster: if not for yourself, then to yourself through those you love. The Stoics try to escape the dilemma by teaching themselves to be untouched by human emotion, as Brutus meets the death of Portia with the words "With meditating that she must die once I have the patience to endure it now." This is to deny to life the right to emotion or to passion, and Augustine, with a surer grasp of what was needed in a conquering faith, is ready to enrol all emotion and all passion in the service of the heavenly City. His hold on men is to be that he is no ascetic by natural temper, but a man alive to the sensuous and varied beauty of material things. "For the beauty and use of other creatures, which God has set before the eyes of man (though as yet miserable and amongst miseries), what man is able to recount them? The universal gracefulness of the heavens, the earth and the sea, the brightness of the light in the sun, moon and stars, the shades of the woods, the colours and smell of flowers, the numbers of birds and their varied hues and songs, the many forms of beasts and fishes, whereof the least are the rarest (for the fabric of the bee or ant is more to be wondered at than the whales); and the strange alterations in the colour of the sea (as though in several garments) now one green, then another, now blue, then purple. . . . Oh, who can enumerate the particulars? How tedious should I be in every particular of these few that I have here as it were heaped together if I should dwell upon them, one by one! Yet are all these but solaces of man's miseries, in no way pertinent to his glories."

In no way pertinent to his glories. And so *The City of God* draws to its close. Augustine, who was to be by his learning and vision the bridge between the ancient world that had passed and the new world as yet without form, who had spent his life in a time of the falling of kingdoms and the breaking of faiths, who·had come to find no meaning in existence unless the Now could be forever and the Forever now, ends with words of longing for "eternal rest of the spirit, but also of the body. There we shall rest and see, we shall see and love, we shall love and we shall praise. . . . For what other thing is our end but to come to that Kingdom of which there is no end?"

LECTURE III

LECTURE III

O NCE upon a time, before men formed themselves into political societies, they lived in a state of nature. Each man in this state had certain natural rights, rights, that is, which belonged to him just because he was a man. They were the rights to life, to liberty and to property. Political societies, States, were formed by mutual arrangement, as business men form mutual insurance societies, to guarantee these rights, because men, uncombined, found it difficult to make their rights secure. This is the only purpose of the State and its only justification, and if those who hold power in it use its power for any other purpose they betray their trust and forfeit the right to hold it.

This, in bare outline, is the famous theory of Natural Rights and the Social Contract. I started it like the opening of a fairy story, because it seems to me just like a fairy story. Yet it is the theory of John Locke, who was that rare thing, an English philosopher; the writer whose essays on *Toleration* and "the true original extent and end of Civil Government" were the inspiration of the Whig party, the man who was able to explain, characteristically, how it was that the English Revolution of 1688 was not really a revolution at all. And the theory bit deep into the minds of those who were later to make the American and the French Revolutions. Indeed, it bit deep into the political structure of the eighteenth and nineteenth centuries and traces of it can be found in unexpected corners today. More than that, the theory of natural rights looks like coming back to us with something of its old apostolic fervour, owing to the rise of American influence in world affairs: for the American

Revolution began with the announcement, as self-evident truth, "that all men are created equal, that they are endowed by their Creator with certain unalienable rights, that among these are Life, Liberty and the Pursuit of Happiness."

Now, as soon as one begins to consider these ideas, several questions come up. Did their sponsors really believe in this original state of nature? I think that they did. I cannot read Locke without thinking that he did. Before the nineteenth century an antiquarian's chief equipment was his imagination, and it is difficult to appreciate how very misty men of the seventeenth century were about all primitive history. Again, did these men really believe that political society is formed by any process at all resembling a voluntary contract? Again, I think, yes. Probably nobody accepts these beliefs today: yet it is often said that the ideas themselves represent something that is still alive and valuable, even if their basis is quite unreal. I would like to look into that.

Certainly, it makes a very pedestrian affair of the State if the whole association is to be thought of as a kind of business contract. Contract and rights: this is to use lawyer's language, and it is true that this particular set of political ideas is largely the creation of lawyers. But, above all, they are ideas designed to lower the status of political power. How it is fallen from its high estate! No longer the supreme mission, responsible for all of everyone's life, as Plato saw it; no longer the divine duty of medieval thought; instead, power is an official confined to his task of making sure that the individual citizen is free to pursue the great end of making the best or most of himself. Here then, is a negative theory about power, a theory intended to tie it down, and a positive theory about the individual, a theory intended to let him loose. Loose for what? I do not think that the answer belongs to this lecture, because the question itself did not directly trouble the men I am speaking of. What mattered to them, above everything else, was that there should be individual liberty.

For Locke was rationalising a change that had come over the world. One must look back to see the nature of this change. The faith and the life of ten centuries had dissolved with the Middle Ages, and they, with their beliefs and fears, had passed away. Men had reclaimed the right to critical thought, and to think critically means, should mean, discovery and invention. The power to criticise, the freedom to discover, to innovate, led to a new self-confidence. Man himself, perhaps, so "noble in reason", so "infinite in faculty", was the lost heir to the world's estate: and that other world, which pressed so close about and intermingled with the life of the Middle Ages, shrank away from these hard and questioning eyes. There is a passage of Pascal that expresses something of the combined grandeur and arrogance of this new attitude. "'Thought," he says, "makes the essence of man; one cannot think of him without it. . . . Man is nothing but a reed, the weakest in all nature; but he is a reed that thinks. It needs no universe in arms to wipe him out: a mist, a drop of water can finish him. Well, if the universe should wipe him out, still man would be nobler than his destroyer, for while he knows his death as he dies, the universe is not even conscious of its triumph over him. All human dignity, then, lies in thought. . . . Let us try to think aright, for right thinking is the basis of morality."

This sense of personal independence, personal responsibility, was reflected in the independent national state. From the fifteenth century onwards, at least, Christendom was in liquidation and its former members began to claim that neither external ruler nor external rule should stand between them and their "manifest destiny". The old ideas of universal order were put away. The first result was to strengthen the grip of secular power. For the holder was at once a tribal chief, embodying his people's hopes and ambitions, and at the same time the only remaining representative of order in the new and pathless wilderness that they were to explore.

Small wonder that this period of dissolution was the period of the extremest doctrines of political obedience. But it is strange to see how these doctrines were upheld by the teaching of those bold men who were working to create the Protestant and Reformed churches. None so absolute as they in civil matters, partly, perhaps, because they were so radical in religion. It was work enough to defy the lightning of Rome. Wycliffe, Luther, Tyndale, each of them can be drawn upon for the most positive instructions of non-resistance to the civil power. "The King," said Tyndale, later to die bravely for his faith at Vilvorde, "is in this world without law and may at his lust do right or wrong and shall give account to God only." "The only right of the Christian," said Luther, "is suffering and the Cross." When the serfs in Suabia revolted, Luther replied to their appeal that their lords had behaved like tyrants and would be judged by God, but they themselves had transgressed against God by their insurrection. This is to turn the doctrine of Divine Right upside down. And our own James I, who could always be trusted to say a silly thing in an arresting way, was there to do it. "If there is an unjust royal command," he explained, "the people may do no other than flee unresistingly from the anger of its King; its tears and sighs are the only answer to him allowed it, and it may summon none but God to its aid."

There is no end to this sort of thing in the seventeenth century. I could match the divines from the philosophers, and find in the greatest of them, Bacon, Descartes, Pascal, Spinoza, the same virtual worship of absolute power, "that Mortal God," as Hobbes called it, "to which we owe under the Immortal God our peace and defence." I cannot explain it, this panic of the soul, for it seizes men who are capable of intrepid conduct as well as of audacity in thought. It seems to be a feeling that civil order is so overwhelming a good that civil obedience becomes the first and highest duty of man, no matter what private conscience or personal morality may say.

Wars of religion had ravaged Western Europe in the sixteenth and seventeenth centuries and men who had lived through those times had reason enough to put peace and order above every other value. That would account for the attitude of practical statesmen such as William Cecil in England and De l'Hopital in France: they had first to disarm the fanatic before their successors would have time even for toleration. But order for the sake of order is a sterile use of power: in the end it can never be adequate as a justification of the State's authority. Some deep internal sense of insecurity must have caught these philosophers and religious leaders of that day: for their appointment should be with time and eternity, not with current politics.

I have seen such a sense of insecurity at work in the world in our generation and it corrupts, though it corrupts subtly, both the rulers and the ruled. And whatever else it does, it elevates political power into a world of its own, in which the rules that govern conduct, if there are any, are not the human rules of right and wrong.

This is the real importance of Machiavelli. People speak of this devoted little Florentine as if his writings contained some dark scheme for debauching public morality. Nothing of the sort. He was an ardent Italian nationalist, sick at heart to see Italy destroyed by the intrigues of other countries, France, Germany, Switzerland, Spain, and by her own dissension. What he wanted above everything was to see Italy strong and united. To gain this there must arise some hero-prince, half-fox, half-lion, who would abjure the accepted rules of moral conduct for himself in order to win freedom for his people; for, says Machiavelli in his *Discourses*, "Where the deliberation is wholly touching the safety of the fatherland there ought to be no consideration of just or unjust, pitiful or cruel, honourable or dishonourable, but rather, all other respect being laid aside, that course ought to be taken which may preserve the life and maintain the life and liberty thereof."

Very likely Machiavelli, who was not at all indifferent to private morality, thought that those who mixed themselves in these high politics would go to Hell for their pains, but he thought the sacrifice was called for to preserve the fatherland. In other words he wanted to do what Cavour succeeded in doing in the nineteenth century, and by methods not so dissimilar; but, whereas Cavour was loudly applauded, because by that time the cause of nationalism had acquired a sanctity of its own, the name of Machiavelli remains as a byword for political cynicism.

In fact, he was no cynic. But having, unlike most political schemers, made no secret of his purpose, he has done himself no good by the candour of his language. If you read *The Prince*, his manual for the private instruction of the saviour-to-be, you need strong nerves. "It is necessary for a prince who desires to preserve himself to be able to make use of honesty or to lay it aside as need shall require." "It must be understood that a prince, and especially a new prince, cannot observe all those things which are considered good in men, being often obliged, in order to maintain the state, to act against faith, against charity, against humanity, and against religion." And, lastly, my two favourites: (1) "it cannot be called virtue to kill one's fellow citizens, betray one's friends, be without faith, without pity and without religion"; and (2) "it is to be noted that, in taking a state, the conqueror must arrange to commit all his cruelties at once, so as not to have to recur to them every day." How candid and how modest all this is after the sanctimonious ideologies to which we are now asked to grow accustomed.

What is disconcerting about Machiavelli is that he cannot be dismissed as altogether in the wrong. Political power cannot be administered as if its actions were merely private dealings between one man and another. In that sense it is not bound by the same rules as those of personal morality: and unless this is realised, altogether too little attention is paid to considering what is the special morality of power. From this two reflections, before I pass on. One, a reinforcement of Plato's theme, that no system can be so important as that which trains and secures the best for the corps of rulers. The other, that other countries may have gone some way to solving what this country has hardly begun to admit. There is, for instance, the work of the Conseil d'État in France. There, in a country in which, traditionally, the acts of the Government and its servants are not subject to the same limitations of law as govern the private citizen, they have developed, not from outside, but within the Government itself, a judicial system that prescribes for its own rules of justice and fair dealing.

Now put the theories of John Locke against this background. The social contract, natural rights, government by consent of the governed : they are all ideas, myths, if you like, which are launched as arguments against absolute power. They were not new ideas ; in fact they are part of the eternal armoury of oppressed against oppressor. Locke and Shaftesbury and their party turned them against James II primarily because he claimed that the King, acting as the executive power, was not bound by the laws of the kingdom and could even exempt his subjects from them.

As ideas they were quite familiar to the Middle Ages, who had used them, more wisely, I think, as good arguments to confound an opponent rather than as the ultimate revelation of truth. The supporters of the Empire had used them against the Papacy, the Papal reformers against the Pope, the Jesuits of the Counter-Reformation against the new Protestant Governments. But it was the peculiar achievement of the eighteenth century and of the school of Locke to make these ideas the theory of government itself.

To my mind they cannot take the strain. They are not enough to account for the demands that the State makes upon individuals, or, for that matter, for the claims that they make upon it. It is a weakness at the heart of the liberal, democratic State that its theory has always been so sober a thing, so much an affair of the counting-house and the share-holders' meeting. When a reckoning is made of its great successes—which may be quite short-lived in terms of history—a large share may be found to be due to a social tradition that is much older than the theory itself, that indeed persisted as a bond of society in spite of the prevailing theory and in opposition to it. But, discount them as you will, these arguments about men being subject only to such government as they consented to, and about their being bound to each other or to the State power by agreement and no more—these arguments suited the times because they suited the energies and opportunities of the day. The grave question of the present time is what value is left in them if the energies and the opportunities of another day take a different course.

It may be useful to bring home to people that all societies hang together in reliance upon some conditions which they regard as the basis of civilised life and that all power in those societies ought to be exercised so as to respect those con-ditions. But surely it is wildly unreal to pretend that such conditions can be expressed with any precision or that they are settled by any process that is at all like a contract. Nowa-days at any rate there is no voluntary agreement involved in being a citizen of a particular State. Virtually all its members belong to it because they were born in it, and long before they were old enough to make a mature decision they had become part of it by the force of family ties, associations, education—in short, men adopt the way of life of a society for almost any other reason than that of deliberate choice. And just because a man's relationship to his country is part of its history and his, the bonds that unite him to it, to its institutions and to his fellow countrymen are far stronger than the obligations of any contract. I cannot improve upon Edmund Burke's comment, when he says, "Society is indeed a contract . . . but the State ought not to be considered as nothing better than a partnership agreement in a trade of pepper and coffee, calico or tobacco or some other such low concern, to be taken up for a little temporary interest and dissolved at the fancy of the parties. . . . It is a partnership in all science; a partnership in all art; a partnership in every virtue, and in all perfection. As the ends of such a partnership cannot be obtained in many generations, it becomes a partnership not only between those who are living, but between those who are living, those who are dead, and those who are to be born." Just so. But if the State does indeed serve purposes so elevated and so all-embracing, what becomes of the theory that it exists only to guarantee certain essential conditions for its members?

These conditions are, according to Locke, their "natural rights". As a general principle Natural Rights do not, I think, get one very far. In its origin the idea is religious and is, in effect, the faith that such conditions are things essential to the making of a human soul. But as an idea it has suffered somewhat from the fact that its development came in a period of rationalism. It does not rationalise easily. For one thing, no one has ever succeeded in settling what these natural rights are. It is all very well for Locke to say that they are life, liberty and property, but he was something of an innovator in introducing "property". To him it was equivalent to the fruits of a man's own labour, though his fellow-Whigs would hardly have been content with so nice a definition. He would have done better to follow Bodin, and to say with him that property is a natural right because the family is the essential unit of ordered society and the family and private property are ideas inseparably connected. The American Declaration of Independence came out for "life, liberty and the pursuit of happiness" as natural rights; the French Declaration of 1789, "life, property, security and resistance to oppression". I could add longer and even vaguer combinations from other sources. I believe that one list included the National Debt among national rights. To cut it short, the list tends to vary with the outlook or literary power of its makers, and, although such rights may be sacred, inalienable or imprescriptible, as they have been variously called, it is a pity that it still remains so uncertain what in fact they are. It is not as if they could be put forward, either, as absolute rights. Only an anarchist could maintain that society may not in any circumstances interfere with, say, a man's life, liberty or property. What we quarrel about is the definition of the circumstances that justify such interference. Now Locke and his school treated this problem as virtually solved so long as you had government by consent, and as their assumptions still prevail in democratic countries, it is worthwhile to give them a glance.

Government by consent of the governed is a very important principle and it runs back to the beginnings of English history. To put it as it was put by Hooker, from whom Locke drew much of his argument, "Laws they are not: for the public approbation hath not made them so." That was one of the constitutional functions that Parliament had acquired: to assent or to refuse consent to laws on behalf of the realm. Members of Parliament have been described as "the King's Physicians . . . with whom he consults". And, of course, you must have representatives for this purpose. They might be chosen or summoned as representatives of the established interests of the country; we have come to a system in which they represent the population of a mere geographical division. But when the representative body advances from the work of accepting or refusing to the work of making and unmaking the laws themselves, displaces the old monarchical power and becomes a sovereign in its own right, does not the theory of consent become a rather insubstantial support for the laws' claim to obedience? Millions of voters, obviously, can be represented in Parliament only by a member whose political views are opposed to theirs; just as electors who favour the minority party can expect to see in the main only legislation to which they object.

I think that Locke takes the theory of consent much too lightly. The truth is that he was a leader of that school of sentimental English and American writers who speak of The People as if it were a single person with one mind and one interest, instead of a complex mass of individuals with different purposes and conflicting interests. To such thinkers the problem is easy: the representative body stands for The People and whatever it decides upon, even by a bare majority, is the Voice of the People. A business-like race, such as the English, gets so accustomed to accepting a majority vote that it sometimes forgets that the majority principle, though unavoidable for handling practical affairs of daily life, is not so obviously right as the only test when it comes to deciding some great issue of social or constitutional policy. It is the weakness of Locke's theory that it raises only the feeblest of barriers to the power of Parliament itself. Apart from a passing compliment to the Law of Nature, which is an "eternal rule" to all legislators, and some good practical advice about not making what he calls " extempore arbitrary decrees" instead of standing laws, he really leaves Parliament in possession of the field. It is to be a master without constitutional limitations, for its purpose is that of "achieving the public good". After all, he reflects, if it betrays this trust and endeavours "to invade the property of the subject and to make themselves, or any part of the community, masters or arbitrary disposers of the lives, liberties or fortunes of the people" (whatever all that means) the people can always have a revolution! The Tsarist Government used to be spoken of as despotism tempered by assassination; similarly, the classical Whig theory might be said to be one of parliamentary absolutism tempered by revolution!

It is only fair to Locke to say that, writing at the end of the seventeenth century, he did not foresee the extent to which the closely organised political party or caucus would invalidate the theory of Parliament that he was so eloquently expounding. It is a very instructive piece of our political history to note how attitudes towards organised party have changed. In the seventeenth and eighteenth centuries organised party was not respectable: it was called faction. It was regarded as unfair to the process of Parliamentary debate ("avoid faction," wrote Chatham's grandfather to his son, "and never enter the House prepossessed: but attend diligently to the debate and vote according to your conscience"). Also it was thought to be faintly seditious, for the King was still very much in politics and the Government in power, his ministers, had something of royalty about them. The seventeenth-century Marquis of Halifax, with whose writings I sometimes refresh myself, is particularly brisk at the expense of Party. "The best party," he says in his *Political Thoughts and Reflections*, "is but a kind of conspiracy against the rest of the Nation. They put everybody else out of their Protection. Like the Jews to the Gentiles, all others are the offscourings of the World."

Of course, we have changed all that long since. With the middle of the nineteenth century the principle of the organised party in political life became accepted. Indeed, it might be truer to say that it became the principle of political life. Few of those actively engaged in politics would accept that you could now conduct the business of Parliament without it. Perhaps a good deal turns upon the degree to which the organisation is carried: for, carried to its logical conclusion, Parliament is turned into the instrument of power, instead of being its holder. But if the obligation of the man of politics is not to begin and end with the duty of playing for his side—and surely it must reach beyond that—there ought to be room on his bookshelves for the writings of George Savile, Marquis of Halifax. Halifax, called the Trimmer, because he put the commonwealth above party. His own essay, *The Character of a Trimmer*, is not ashamed to claim his title. Not a romantic man, or a sentimental man, or a great partisan, or a great hater: but a brave, cool-headed, independent Englishman, who knew only one theme for eloquence. I will let him speak. "Our Trimmer is far from idolatry in other things, in one thing only he cometh near it, his Country is in some degrees his Idol; he doth not worship the Sun, because 'tis not peculiar to us, it rambles about the world and is less kind to us than others; but for the Earth of England, tho' perhaps inferior to that of many places abroad, to him there is Divinity in it and he would rather die than see a spire of English grass trampled down by a foreign trespasser."

LECTURE IV

LECTURE IV

IT seems to me a reasonable proposition that the making of the American Constitution was one of the most important events in modern history. It was important, to begin with, that the Constitution was a made thing: that it was debated and voted upon clause by clause and finally written down and accepted as the whole set of political rules that were to govern the future of the United States of America. You can take that set of rules in your hand today, including all the amendments that have been made since, and in half an hour you can read everything that is in them, though I do not say that you will comprehend all that it amounts to. It was the first Constitution of modern history that was worked out and reduced to writing, unlike our own, for instance, which has never gone through any such clarifying process; and it is a great deal more comprehensible, not merely because it is shorter, than some other more elaborate written Constitutions that have been produced since then.

Next, it was a Federal Constitution, again the pioneer of its kind. The men who founded it were quite aware that in this they were giving a new political conception to the world, a conception that can be explained in this way. Separate Sovereign States were so far to combine with each other as to secure that each would be neither wholly independent nor wholly merged: but certain interests common to them all, defence, foreign relations, trade policy, were to be dealt with exclusively by a new central authority, and where those matters were concerned the citizens of the States became directly subjects of this authority. That remains the

situation in the United States today. The separate States that
make up the Union retain their sovereignty for all purposes
that they have not surrendered to the Federal Government,
and an American has, as it were, his dual citizenship, local
and national. When one reads *The Federalist*, the series of
eighty-five essays that were published in New York State to
explain and defend the proposed Constitution, one sees that
the Founding Fathers had searched the history of ancient
Greece and Rome, and were learned about the affairs of the
Amphictyonic League and the Lycian Confederacy and the
Achaean League, and had searched the history of Europe and
knew all about the United Netherlands, the Holy Roman
Empire and the Swiss Cantons; but all these examples they
rejected as unsatisfactory on the ground that they were mere
confederacies, mere unions of sovereign States which asso-
ciated as States without surrendering any part of their
sovereignty over their own citizens. The Americans themselves had been working under an arrangement of this kind
from the beginning of the War of Independence and they
had seen that a central authority which has to rely upon its
member States to carry its decisions into effect and which
cannot make its laws directly binding upon the citizens of
those States is a kind of authority that is doomed to impotence.
"Influence is not government," was George Washington's
summary of its failure. Those who framed and supported the
new Constitution had no use for such an authority: and the
scheme that they worked out for the union of their thirteen
States has been the prototype whenever since then men have
had to consider the problems of a Federal Union. For instance, you can see how strongly it affected the form of the
Canadian and Australian constitutions when they came to be
made, though each is very far from being a copy of the
American. I read Hamilton's arguments in *The Federalist*
today: and at every page I am interested by their bearing
upon the structure of the United Nations, or indeed of

any of the proposed federations that are now talked
about. "Make up your minds as to what you really want,"
he seems to say. "That is the first essential thing. If
you really think it best to place this or that branch of
your affairs under the authority of some larger union,
then give it frankly the powers it needs to make its control
effective. Do not be afraid or half-hearted in what you are
doing, or take back with one hand what you give with the
other."

It seems to me a singular piece of fortune that we have this
opportunity of watching a remarkable group of men debating
the very basis, purpose and limitations of political power.
Remarkable they certainly were. No one can read Madison's
record of those summer months at Philadelphia in 1787
without being struck by the learning and sense of statesmanship that were shown by many of the delegates who were
there to frame the Constitution. They included most of the
leading figures in American life: except Thomas Jefferson,
who was mercifully away in Paris. For Jefferson, sentimental,
uncertain, unprincipled, was not the stuff of which Constitutions are made. In their way the *Federalist* papers are even
more remarkable than the Philadelphia debates: for they
were produced, primarily at any rate, for the general public
of New York State, to persuade them to ratify the proposals
and they were, it seems, only one, though much the best, of
many publications of the same sort. The historical and
classical allusions, the grave reasonableness, the careful
analysis of detail and sound basis of general principle might
well lead you to think that they were addressed to a college
of professors. Yet the population of New York State then, as
now, was very unlike a college of professors. One is left to
conclude that the three million free white men, who were
reckoned to make up the population of the thirteen States,
were something like a nation of statesmen. That is why they
got such a good Constitution.

Not that it was easily come by. Most of the States contained resolute opponents of the new federal power that the Constitution was to set up. Opposition was particularly strong in New York State itself, and no one ever has been quite clear how it was that the large hostile majority in the State Convention was in the end brought to vote for ratification, except that Alexander Hamilton, tireless and overwhelming in debate, had determined that it should. Opposition might base itself on what were called State Rights—which meant, in effect, "We can look out for ourselves best by keeping the whole sovereign power in our existing State and not sharing any of it with others"—or it might base itself on misgivings as to how far this new federal power, representing all the States, might be found overriding the interests of any one State. For instance, with the federal government controlling all import tariffs and some of the northern States favouring protection, what might happen to a State in the South that depended on exporting its raw materials and importing manufactures in exchange? But whatever form opposition took, it came back somehow or other to this main question, Had the federal power been created in such a form that it would be likely to prove too strong for the liberties of the people? The three joint authors of *The Federalist*, Madison, Hamilton and Jay, set themselves to give a convincing answer to this question, and the great interest of these papers to-day lies, I think, in their handling of the answer. They were men whose own services, at any rate, were to be given to the new Constitution. Madison was to serve two terms as President of the United States, Hamilton was the first Secretary of its Treasury, Jay the first Chief Justice of the Supreme Court and envoy extraordinary to England.

There was one principle of government that seems to have been held in common by both advocates and opponents. At least, I cannot find that at Philadelphia anyone challenged it, and *The Federalist* assumes it as something beyond argument.

That principle is known as the Separation of Powers, and it formed the very foundation of the American Constitution. It had an interesting history. In the eighteenth century the British Constitution provoked very general admiration outside the country. Our combination of effective government with political liberties was much envied and it was held that these liberties enjoyed a special security because we kept our three branches of authority, the law-making, the executive and the judicial, separate and independent of each other, so that each, it was said, checked and balanced the other and thereby preserved the liberties of the individual citizen. It was founded, as you see, on the assumption that unless you divided up political power in a State among equal independent authorities the one chief authority would be sure to abuse its powers. It is usual, I believe, to say that the theory completely misread the real situation in England and that the Americans were following a will-o'-the-wisp when they adopted it. But, to begin with, I am not sure that that is quite right. Certainly the judges played an important part throughout the eighteenth century in upholding individual rights against encroachment by the executive. By the beginning of the century they had been placed in a position that made them free from interference by Crown or Parliament, and Parliament had not then begun the practice of passing statutes that give the executive a safe conduct through the ordinary law. The relations between Crown and Parliament are more difficult to analyse and it needs an expert in the period to decide which controlled which, if each was not independent of the other. Conditions varied with different reigns, but at least it is true that throughout the century the king had the means and power of deciding which of the two main political groups he would place in office. That is, at least, a kind of independence.

But, whether right or wrong about England, the Americans accepted the theory of separation of powers as an obvious truth. The idea of letting one branch accumulate in its hands all the important "prerogatives of sovereignty" struck them as something that no sane statesman could possibly allow. That, said *The Federalist*, would be to "entail upon our posterity one of the most execrable forms of government that human infatuation ever contrived". It is to this belief that the American Constitution owes its most characteristic features. Laws can only be made by the agreement of two Houses, the members of one elected from the States in proportion to population and by popular suffrage, the members of the other consisting of two senators for each State, also, since 1913, elected. The whole of the executive power of the Union is in the hands of the President, but he does not belong to either house of Congress nor is he chosen through them: he is elected, in effect, directly by the people of the Union. The members of his Cabinet, his ministers, are not allowed to be members of either House any more than he is. The President has a power of veto over any measures of the two Houses, even when they are agreed; but they can override his veto if two thirds of the members of each House are still in favour of their measure. The Supreme Court, though its members are appointed by the President, has no connection with the Legislature or the Executive and the judges are irremovable during good behaviour.

English critics of the American Constitution have been inclined to concentrate on the rigidity which does necessarily result from keeping the executive body and the law-making body so much at arm's length. They have lamented the fact that under such a system there can quite well be, and sometimes has been, stalemate between President and Congress or between one House of Congress and the other. When that happens no side has such sovereign power as enables it to override its opponent. How unlike indeed the situation that we have now reached in this country, in which there is absolutely nothing that cannot be enacted and made into law within a comparatively short space of time by a bare numerical majority in the House of Commons.

But it was not the Constitution's rigidity that troubled American opponents at the time. Nor did they object to the obvious fact that it was ill adapted to respond at short notice to what the "voice of the people" might be thought to be saying. On the contrary, it was regarded as a very democratic instrument. Most of its makers could be classed as sincere friends of the people (to use the phrase of the day), even if Hamilton himself spoke of the people as "a great beast" and John Adams, Washington's successor as President, once wrote "The People . . . unchecked . . . is as unjust, tyrannical, brutal, barbarous and cruel as any King or Senate possessed of an uncontrolled power." In fact, Jefferson's easy maxims that all men are naturally good, if only governments do not interfere by governing, and that each man is as good as the next—these maxims were very well in their place, which is the backwoods; but few, if any, of the Founding Fathers supposed that you could conduct the affairs of a great State without authority or that authority, though it might be wise to divide it up, ought not to be strong in its own sphere. Washington was to say in his Farewell Address, some years later: "Remember especially that for the efficient management of your common interest in so extensive a country a government of as much vigour as is consistent with the perfect security of liberty is indispensable. Liberty itself will find in such a government, with powers properly distributed and adjusted, its surest guardian." That was what all Federalists wanted; but how much vigour of government was consistent with the perfect security of liberty?

It is interesting to see how Madison handles this subject in *The Federalist*. His was probably the biggest single influence in the framing of the Constitution and everything that he says in Papers 47 to 51 is worth attention to-day. He starts, of course, with the same assumption as they all made, that the very definition of tyranny consists in accumulating all powers in the same hands and that it makes no sort of difference for this purpose whether the hands are hereditary, self-appointed or elected. He shows, without much difficulty, that this principle has never meant that the various powers must be kept absolutely distinct from each other; what it really means is that the whole power of one branch of State authority must not be exercised by another or its whole administration conducted under the influence of another. For instance, he would say, the Executive, the branch that administers or carries out the laws, must not be dominated by, nor must it in its turn dominate, the Legislature, the branch that makes the laws—you need separate wills, not one will. So you must frame your Constitution in such a way that each can maintain a substantial share of independence. But merely to define each department's separate status is to erect what he calls "parchment barriers". Power is of "an encroaching spirit" and the legislative department, he notes, is "everywhere extending the sphere of its activity and drawing all power into its impetuous vortex". He treats this as a general rule in all states that maintain representative government, if only because of the prestige that popular election is supposed to give. I think he is right in that, and that there is much force in his comment that in America the men who had drawn up new constitutions for the individual States had been obsessed with the danger to liberty presented by a hereditary monarch and a hereditary Upper House. In the result they had quite forgotten to provide against usurpations by a legislature, which can lead to just the same tyranny. I sometimes think that in this country we still speak as if our main duty was to guard our Constitution against James II, whereas in fact the conditions have long passed away in which the Executive can threaten civil liberties unless it has Parliament behind it. "It is one thing", says Hamilton in a later paper, "to be subordinate to the laws and another to be dependent on the legislative body."

How, then, was the Constitution to make sure that the individual citizen in the Union would not be at the mercy of its legislature's law-making powers? Madison examines various devices that might help to fortify the parchment barriers: but in the end he says, not very hopefully as it seems to me, that the best security is to give each of the branches of government, legislative, executive and judicial, constitutional means and personal motives that will lead it to resist encroachments from another. Well, prestige and a sense of office will generally supply the personal motive and I suppose that the President's veto on legislation is the kind of thing that Madison meant by constitutional means of defence. But his general apology seems to show that in the end he regards this as a question outside any Constitution. "It may be a reflection on human nature that such devices should be necessary to control the abuses of government. But what is government itself but the greatest of all reflections on human nature? If men were angels, no government would be necessary. If angels were to govern men, neither external nor internal controls in government would be necessary. In framing a government which is to be administered by men over men, the great difficulty lies in this: you must first enable the government to control the governed; and in the next place oblige it to control itself."

If Madison is driven to descend to generalities when he speaks of obliging a government to control itself, both he and Hamilton were very clear about the danger from faction. They both saw that faction, by which they meant "self-seeking" party, can wreck any constitutional theory, since it uses the forms of the Constitution to defeat the Constitution's purpose. Faction was the great danger of the early Union, which was a raw mixture of classes, interests and even sects, any one of which might capture power to serve a purely selfish end. Madison did not deny that this was likely. The causes of faction, he said, cannot be removed, since selfishness is endemic in human nature. What you must aim to do is to control its effects: not by moral or religious appeals, which will never be adequate, nor by reducing people to a perfect equality in political rights, which still leaves them with different possessions, opinions and passions; but in part by relying on the representatives of the people to have a mind wiser and juster than that of the people themselves, and in part by drawing your representatives from as wide and varied an area as is possible. That, of course, is an argument for the Union. "Extend the sphere," he says, "and you take in a greater variety of parties and interests; you make it less probable that a majority of the whole will have a common motive to invade the rights of other citizens." And that circumstance, the comparative looseness of organisation and vagueness of design that the great area of the United States has forced on its national parties, is, if I do not mistake contemporary American historians, the main cause why it has been spared some of the worst results of faction.

Many people thought that no Constitution could be complete that did not contain a Bill of Rights. They meant by this a list of civil rights to be guaranteed by the Constitution. The idea was familiar. Several of the new State Constitutions contained such lists, and at the back there were always the invigorating words of the Declaration of Independence, that men were created equal and endowed by their Creator with certain unalienable rights, including Life, Liberty and the Pursuit of Happiness. No one could be very sure what these words meant or how far they were supposed to go; but they were something to start from. The British Constitution was thought to be founded upon the Bill of Rights which Parliament had presented to William and Mary after the Revolution and then made into an Act of Parliament. Edmund Burke was teaching everyone to regard the Revolutionary Settlement as the final and unalterable form of the British Constitution, and Thomas Paine, who was perhaps of the two the one rather more read in America, had not yet written his *Rights of Man* to show that in the American sense there was no British Constitution at all. For all the great instruments of our history, Magna Carta, the Petition of Right, the Bill of Rights, were essentially treaties between the monarch on the one hand and some other power, the feudal lords, or Parliament, on the other. Parliament had put into its Act containing the Bill of Rights provisions about juries and freedom of election and excessive bail, and restriction on Royal prerogative. But what Parliament had put into one Act, it could alter or remove by another Act.

The authors of *The Federalist* knew that this lack of a Bill of Rights was one of the strongest criticisms of their new Constitution. They tried to meet it by saying that it was really there all the time. What they had in mind was that in a Federal Constitution you must by the necessity of the thing be precise as to what can and what cannot be done by one or other of the bodies between whom you are going to distribute the powers of sovereignty. Federation is a kind of treaty and the parties to it stipulate their conditions. These conditions are a kind of safeguard. For instance, the American Constitution makes a detailed list of the subjects upon which Congress is to be able to make laws. An Act of Congress that dealt with some other subject than these would not be an exercise of any power given to it and would be a nullity. But more than this, certain things are forbidden to the federal power and certain things to the individual States and certain things to both of them. That means that it does not matter how much public opinion may be said to desire a measure which violates the Constitution, it does not matter that the President and every member of every House might be in favour of it, it cannot be made the law of the land, unless the difficult and laborious business of getting an amendment of the Constitution to allow it has first been gone through. In point of fact the next thing that happened, three years after the Constitution

was adopted, was that ten amendments were added to it
containing the Bill of Rights (so they are called) that the
critics had been calling for. Thus an American can know that
he has certain individual rights which stand above ordinary
laws, things that he cannot be made to submit to by any law:
just as instances, he cannot be subject to any Bill of attainder
or *ex-post-facto* law, he cannot be made to find excessive bail
or excessive fines, or be subjected to cruel or unusual punish-
ments; the federal power cannot pass any law establishing
religion or prohibiting the free exercise of religion, or
abridging the freedom of speech or of the Press.

I could go on, for there are many others, some of which
have proved of great importance. But no one of them seems
to me of as much importance as the principle itself. The
principle has arisen, perhaps, as a by-product of a federal
scheme and a written Constitution, but in the result it has
produced the most effective barrier against encroachments of
power that has been thrown up by the political science of the
modern world. For it has not proved a mere parchment
barrier. Statutes that violate the limitations of the Constitution are not bad laws: they are not laws at all. They are not
laws that still have to be obeyed, even if with protest or
resentment: they are words that can be ignored with im-
punity. It is the medieval doctrine over again, a supreme law
that overrules the law-making of men, but with the written
words of the Constitution in place of the uncertain theories
of Natural Law. I must not make it too simple. It is likely to
be a pretty abstruse question whether a particular statute
violates or complies with the Constitution: it will have to be
taken to the Supreme Court to be decided. But its decision
closes the matter, and in that sense its judges are the final
arbiters of what laws may be passed in America to deal with
many of its most critical affairs.

The same is true of laws passed in Canada and Australia,
and for the same reason, that they have written Federal

Constitutions. Within recent years the Federal Legislature in Australia has passed measures nationalising the banks and suppressing the Communist Party; but both these measures have fallen to the ground because the judges of the High Court of Australia have declared them to be outside the powers of that Legislature.

It does not seem certain that the founders of the Constitution appreciated that they were vesting in the Supreme Court this extraordinary power of annulling legislation. I have not traced any mention of it during the debates at Philadelphia, and the authors of *The Federalist* make no point about it. It was some fifteen years before any case arose which made an issue of the question. Possibly the Supreme Court's claim to have the determining word might not have been established then had not the Chief Justice of that Court turned out to be the famous John Marshall, who pronounced uncompromisingly, "It is emphatically the province and duty of the judicial department to say what the law is." This vast, though unimpeachable, claim shocked many of his contemporaries. It shocked Jefferson particularly: the judiciary of the United States were, he said "a subtle corps of sappers and miners constantly working underground to undermine the foundations of our confederated fabric." But then Jefferson was a man who liked vague sentiments and noble generalities, and that was not the spirit of the men who made the Constitution of the United States. Whatever else it is, it is at any rate the work of men who sought to say clearly what they meant and were ready to abide the consequences.

They could fairly claim that they had done the work of pioneers. And the history of the United States has shown that their theories were not to be defeated by the stubbornness of facts. They were rather sober, lawyer-like business theories of government: but they were going to work according to their terms. First, these men had created a form of popular and democratic government, without placing it at the mercy of its electors. Secondly, they believed that if the branches of government were kept separate individual citizens would be less exposed to its interference; and, despite the creaking and straining that such a system produces, the United States have shown that it can work. Thirdly they showed how individual rights could be made into a law overriding even the decisions of a popular legislature. The rights defined at any rate were guaranteed, even if such rights do not represent the whole, or even perhaps the most important, of man's essential claims. Lastly they were the true authors of the federal idea by which a man can remain a loyal citizen of two different sovereign bodies, so long as their functions are separate and their basic purposes unite.

LECTURE V

LECTURE V

THE British have formed the habit of praising their institutions, which are sometimes inept, and of ignoring the character of their race, which is often superb. In the end they will be in danger of losing their character and being left with their institutions: a result disastrous indeed. I am moved to say this when I consider the strange story of the British Empire in India: an administrative achievement which was unique of its kind, which had every argument against its success except the personal quality of those who took part in it and of which the names of the original founders are virtually forgotten. Tonight I will recall a few of those names. For one reason because the connoisseur of human character will find in them collector's pieces, and for another, because the whole adventure deserves its chapter in the Anatomy of Power. It represents an episode that has been finally closed: and it may well stand as a classic example of how men really respond to the stimulus of great authority.

For these men exercised absolute power. It came into our hands suddenly and it came without qualification or restriction. In 1750 the British in India were a company of merchants clinging, not always successfully, to their main trading posts at Bombay, Madras and Calcutta. By 1850, with the overthrow of the Sikh Kingdom in the Punjab, the Company and the British Government between them were the undisputed masters of India. They had had to fight for their position: against the French, against the provincial governors of the dying Mogul Empire, against Hyder Ali and Tippoo in the South, against the Mahrattas in Central India, against the Gurkhas in Nepal, and, lastly, against the Sikhs in the North

West. There were wars of aggression, there were punitive wars, there were wars of self-defence; but, whatever their purposes, they were generally conducted against the fervent protests of the trading Company, whose directors lacked the taste for military glory. So did some, but not all, of the Governor-Generals supplied to them by British Cabinets in London. For since Parliament had intervened in the Company's affairs by passing Pitt's India Act of 1784 the arrangement had been that the Government in effect appointed the Governor-General, nominated a Board of Control in London, and supplied a modicum of British troops for service in India; while the Company's directors in Leadenhall Street were left in the actual control of their increasingly enormous territories, which they had both to administer and defend. This meant a civil service and armies of their own, apart from trading activities to further what they called their "investment".

It is hardly a matter for surprise that the Company's first essays in administration were quite disastrous. It was the eighteenth century, when even at home, under the un-enthusiastic gaze of their own countrymen, members of the governing class treated bribery and corruption as normal incidents of political life. And the Company's own system asked for trouble. The directors expected their servants to be traders at one moment and government officials the next, and, incidentally, provided them with salaries so low as to amount to no salary at all. This was the era of the Nabobs, servants of the Company who used their position and the power it gave them to extract huge fortunes for their personal use. Even to-day their transactions seem impressive. In Madras, which was never the goldmine for Nabobs that Bengal proved, one official was said to have had £1,200,000 sterling in bribes from the Nawab of the Carnatic; another pocketed £200,000. Clive himself was a man whom it would have been difficult to reward too highly, so immense were his services; but, even so, his actual takings were on the heroic scale. He said later that, when he thought of what he could have had, he "was amazed at his own moderation". But that was not the aspect that struck his contemporaries in India. It was all the more annoying for them, feathering their humbler nests, that he should have returned to Calcutta a stern and entirely sincere critic of lax administration. "Corruption, Licentiousness and Want of Principle seem to have possessed the minds of all the Civil Servants," he wrote, "—they have grown callous, rapacious and luxurious beyond conception."

Both Clive and Warren Hastings, himself far above personal bribery, were genuinely anxious to improve the civil system and to protect the native subject from oppression. They would have liked to realise the Company's earlier instructions to its supervisors in Bengal that they were to stand between the peasant and "the hand of oppression" and to be "his refuge and the redress of his wrongs". But both Clive and Hastings had compromised themselves too deeply in the tangled politics of eighteenth-century India to be very convincing as moral reformers. It needed the new century and a new hand to start the astonishing reformation that was due to take place. The new hand was to be that of a very honest and single-minded gentleman, the Lord Cornwallis.

Cornwallis came out to India as Governor-General at the age of forty eight. He was a man without personal ambition, whose eyes turned back with regret to his children and his honourable retirement in England. "Let me know that you are well and are doing well," he wrote to them, "and I can be happy even in Calcutta." He had no personal leaning towards office work: "My life at Calcutta is perfect clockwork," he told his small son, ".... I do not think the greatest sap at Eton can lead a duller life." But with his good heart and his strong sense of duty he was destined to be the real founder of the Indian Civil Service. He saw that the civil servant, if he was to have even a chance of avoiding temptation, must be reasonably well paid; so he got them proper salaries. In return he required that they must give up all connection with trade; though it was not until 1833 that the Company as a whole became a purely administrative service. He issued a set of Regulations which formed, as it were, the outline of British civil government in India. No doubt they were a good deal too much on Western lines, but thereafter, in those provinces where the Regulations were applied, the civil servant had something rather more than his own unaided discretion to rule by. Lastly—and here comes the decisive break with the eighteenth century—Cornwallis would give no ear to social or political influence in appointments to his service. The Company had begun its career with the austere resolution "not to employ any gentleman in any place of charge". This may have shown too great an attachment to business ethics; but, whatever the intention, by the middle of the eighteenth century the English governing classes had discovered the great possibilities of an Indian appointment in disposing of an embarrassed—or an embarrassing—relative. The prospects were more lucrative than anything that could be wrung out of the English or Irish establishments. Besides, the relative was further away. In one year the list of civil servants in Bengal alone included the names of one peer, nineteen sons of peers and twelve baronets! Cornwallis saw to it that social jobbery of this kind ended under his rule.

Thus the way was clear for the remarkable group of men who were now to govern India. There is a passage of Macaulay in which, after speaking of the "doubtful splendour" of Hastings and Clive, he praises the "spotless glory of Elphinstone and Munro". I will quote his passage, for it tells the whole story. "They are men", he says, "who after ruling millions of subjects, after commanding victorious armies, after dictating terms of peace at the gates of hostile capitals, after administering the revenues of great provinces, after judging the causes of wealthy Zemindars, after residing at the Courts of tributary Kings, return to their native land with no more than a decent competence." From now on those were the terms which the Indian service had to offer: separation, perhaps for good, from home and family; isolation amongst an alien people; heat, discomfort, sickness and often enough an early death by violence or disease. And in return, the chance of unlimited advancement, adventure, power, responsibility—and a decent competence. These terms were not to alter materially until the nineteenth century was far advanced.

And who were the Elphinstone and Munro of Macaulay's speech? Each ended his career as the governor of a great Indian province. One was the fourth son of a Scottish peer, the other (Munro) the son of a Glasgow merchant. Too poor to pay for his passage, he had worked his way out to Madras as an ordinary seaman. John Malcolm and Charles Metcalfe were two other leaders of this first generation. Malcolm was the son of a farmer in Dumfries; Metcalfe's father, on the other hand, had made a fortune in Bengal in the old days and returned to England, to a baronetcy and a seat in Parliament. Their origins illustrate what was to be an outstanding feature of the service: it was genuinely egalitarian and it was recruited in the main from the middle class, who found the social structure at home too unyielding to offer their children any comparable opportunity. These boys came out to India as little more than children—fifteen or sixteen was the ruling age. Likely as not their families would not see them again and parting was often final. Home leave would come only after years of service or in the case of very serious ill health. There is an entry in the diary of Henry Lawrence's mother which records his return on sick leave after the 1st Burma War "returned from Arakan after the Burmese War my dearest beloved Henry Montgomery, not twenty-one years old, but reduced by sickness and suffering to more than double that age." It is an entry of a type that the British race has grown all too familiar with.

The whole system seems casual enough. Its success is eloquent of the fine material that could be picked, as it were, out of the bag. There were no qualifying examinations at this period, and a cadet entered the civil service or the Company's army on the nomination of one of the directors. That meant an uncle or a family friend or a friend of a family friend. True, the aspirant had an interview with the directors at India House, but at the age of twelve it is not easy to convey convincingly your qualifications as a future Indian Governor or Sepoy General. Not all twelve-year-olds could do themselves such justice as John Malcolm, who answered a director's question, "My little man, what would you do if you went to meet Hyder Ali?" "Do? Why, sir, I would out with my sword and cut off his head."

Once accepted, a cadet in the artillery or engineers had a two-year course of training at Addiscombe, a civilian cadet at the Company's new college at Haileybury; but a cadet in the infantry or cavalry betook himself to India without further preparation. A year later he would find himself in command of men, doing anything or nothing. For in those early years two things are noticeable. The distinction between soldier and civilian was blurred: soldiers became diplomats and administrators, civilians transformed themselves into soldiers. Indeed Elphinstone, whose training for warfare was probably confined to the study of his favourite author Thucydides, actually conducted the successful battle of Khirkee, though discreetly attributing the credit to the aged military commander. Secondly, it was the age of young men. It seems almost ridiculous to read of Metcalfe, a junior in the Political Service, though admittedly an old Etonian, sent at the age of nineteen to negotiate the withdrawal of the armies of Holkar, the formidable Mahratta chief. They got on splendidly. He was only twenty-three when he led a mission to Lahore to treat with Ranjit Singh, the "Lion of the Punjab". He had to wait, but he got his treaty of friendship, an act of great importance for the consolidation of British power in India. After that Elphinstone, at thirty, seems almost a veteran when he goes as our envoy to treat with Shah Sujah at Cabul. Still, the close of his address to the Afghan King is probably a fair sample of the spirit in which these young men advanced upon their extraordinary tasks: "I concluded by saying that we had often been at war with all the world and had never suffered in the contest."

Perhaps one ought not to generalise from a few outstanding men. But the whole lot of them were only a handful. Certain qualities seem to have been common. They had fine nerve and they had fine courage: cold courage that kept men doing brave things, year in, year out, without the expectation of what they did being praised or even recorded. They had, pre-eminently, a sense of duty. They were given absolute power, in effect with no one to control them, often enough judges in their own cause: and they were strong enough not to abuse it. I do not mean merely that they did not, as their immediate predecessors had done, use their power to obtain benefit for themselves. More than that, they really meant to use their power for the benefit of the people whose government had fallen into their hands. Two of the best of them, Outram and Metcalfe, each risked his whole career in fighting what he thought was injustice in the Government's treatment of native rulers. Above all, perhaps, these men kept their heads cool and their hearts open among all the splendours that surrounded them. What made that the more remarkable was that they had no inherited tradition of authority to support them. "The account of your employment is like fairy-tales to us," wrote John Malcolm's father from Dumfries. The "employment" had been as Ambassador to Persia, but his father did not refrain from a piece of parental advice: "A good head will gain you the esteem and applause of the world, but a good heart alone gives happiness to the owner of it."

India in those days roused in our men the sense of wonder that a strange country rouses in an explorer. They were inquisitive, fascinated, if sometimes repelled. The chaos and misery that they found provoked their sense of order, their latent capacity for government; but the spectacle did not make them contemptuous or hostile. Instead they became painstaking historians, they composed Persian grammars, they wrote great double-decker volumes of travel. The most active seem to have found time to write most: Malcolm, with his *Central India* and *History of Persia*, Elphinstone with his massive *History of India*, Outram, *The Conquest of Scinde*. Tod's *History of the Rajputs* remains a classic. Herbert Edwardes' *A Year on the Punjab Frontier* is remarkable on several counts: the personality of the author, the people he had to deal with and his extraordinary gift of writing. The travel books of Alexander Burnes and Arthur Connolly had a great vogue in their day. Both were young officers of the Company's military service. They explored young and died early, Burnes, at thirty-six, cut to pieces by an Afghan mob, Connolly, at thirty-five, put to death with his friend Stoddart at Bokhara, after long imprisonment, ' resolved," as he wrote in his Bible, "please God, to wear our English honesty and dignity to the last."

Increasingly, as the second generation came along, the generation of the Lawrences and Nicholson and Herbert Edwardes and Alexander Taylor, the men who settled the Punjab, there was a fiery devotion to duty, which wore them out before their time. Taylor, an engineer subaltern of twenty-four and a road-builder of genius, wrote long afterwards: "There was a glow of work and duty around us in the Punjab such as I have never felt before or since. I well remember the reaction of feeling when I went on furlough to England: the want of pressure of any kind, the self-seeking, the dulling and dwarfing lack of high aims." There were others who felt as he did. "We have agreed not to recommend any leave except when men are sick," wrote John Lawrence to the Viceroy, ". . . There is still so much to do. Every day is of value, and the best officer cannot work too hard or too long for the public interest."

And yet, between these two generations, there is perceptible a difference in their approach to the nature of our rule. The difference was to be of importance for the future. None of them doubted that British rule could bring great benefits—peace, order, security, protection—to the individual Indian or that it was our duty to stay in India until the natives could provide those benefits for themselves. Looking back, one can see that it was easier to get in than to get out on those terms. That attitude was natural enough in those who had seen the anarchy of the decaying Mogul Empire. But the older school were much more sensitive than their successors to the value of supporting the long-established features of Indian society. They saw that a power, however benevolent, that could not work through the existing forms of that society must prove in the end a destructive force. The old authorities would be put aside, robbed of power and of prestige, and the elements of society would be so levelled out that there would be nothing between Government on the one hand and individual unit, peasant or trader, on the other. That is the classic path to despotism. Where they got this profound truth from, I do not know. They had no administrative history to guide them, and their schooling had been casual. Possibly they had the eighteenth century's instinctive aristocratic feeling. But if anyone wants to read an essay on the art of humane and sensitive administration, I would recommend a study of the letters exchanged between Sir Thomas Munro in Madras and the Company in London during the early years of the nineteenth century. Incidentally, it is excellent writing: appropriately enough on the side of the Company, who were before long to count Thomas Love Peacock and John Stuart Mill at the head of their secretariat, but few of the early Indian administrators seem capable of writing badly. Munro's message is always to the same effect: "Your rule is alien, and it can never be popular. You have much to bring to your subjects, but you cannot look for more than passive gratitude. You are not here to turn India into England or Scotland. Work through, not in spite of, native systems and native ways with a prejudice in their favour rather than against them; and when in the fulness of time your subjects can frame and maintain a worthy Government for themselves, get out and take the glory of the achievement and the sense of having done your duty as the chief reward for your exertions." No wonder that his system was spoken of as "a reign of affection instead of law". No wonder that, a hundred years after he died of cholera in camp in India, his word was still law and a revenue officer noted that you had only to say that some rule had been laid down by Munro to end all argument upon it.

The younger school lost something of Munro's sensitive patience. They were terrific men—remorseless in energy and in their devotion to duty—but they were almost dangerously sure that they were right and that their principles were so superior that nothing ought to stand in the way of their being immediately enforced. They saw themselves, not unjustly, as the protectors of the oppressed cultivator and small man, but in their enthusiasm every one who stood between them and their charge—the chieftain, big or small, the landlord, the middleman—was not only thrust aside but was likely to be regarded as morally deplorable as well. "Eschew middlemen," said John Lawrence to Nicholson; "they are the curse of the country everywhere." But an ancient and complex society cannot be simplified to this extent without losing in the process something that is part of its life itself. Nor is there any time-sheet upon which can be entered the value of human personality. "A naked people under a naked crown" is the description of a despotism, however benevolent and high-minded the despot himself. And it was in this sense that the British rule in India came to be called despotic.

In a sense the great achievement of British rule in this period, the settlement of the land revenue, was calculated to encourage just this tendency to direct personal rule. The central problem of Indian administration was the settlement of the land. So it must be in a country where agriculture was the great source of wealth and of Government revenue. But the land system had broken down in much of India during generations of disorder. To settle these vast and unmapped territories meant to survey them, to record them, to decide the million questions of disputed title that arose in connection with them and to assess the holdings for purposes of revenue. There was hardly one of our leading officers in India, from Munro and Elphinstone onwards, who was not employed in this exacting labour. It meant a personal attention to detail on the part of the Government that was unknown before, unless perhaps in the greatest days of the Mogul Empire. British Governments had come to favour, rightly or wrongly, a direct assessment by the revenue officer of every holding or at least of every village, instead of the earlier practice of assessing the landlord and leaving him to deal with the cultivators on his own responsibility. Indian critics have said that our system left the cultivator too directly in the hands of Government. But at least it taught the British officer to know India and the Indian peasant as he could never have known them otherwise. It was said of Thomason, Governor of the North West Province and one of the greatest settlement officers, that "there was hardly a place or a road in an area of 70,000 square miles, scarcely a clan or a tribe in a population of 30 millions with which he was not acquainted."

Against much of this, for all its excellence, stands the figure of Henry Lawrence. Indeed his quarrel with his brother John over the policy of administration in the new province of the

Punjab dramatises the conflict between the old school and
the new. Henry lost, when Dalhousie, the Viceroy, supported
John and sent Henry into retirement as agent in Rajputana.
But he took with him the passionate admiration of such iron
men as his own subordinates, John Nicholson and Herbert
Edwardes, and, more than that, the grief and the devotion of
his Indian subjects. "It was a long living funeral procession
from Lahore nearly to Amritsar", someone who saw it said
of his departure. In truth, the conflict was a conflict of attitude as much as of policy. Henry, imaginative and poetical,
could not envisage power under John's simple categories. He
thought that it was our duty to restore and govern through
the Sikh chieftains as a native aristocracy and that there was
no future in India for a government that reserved all high
authority and emolument for itself and reduced all below it to
a common level. A man of profound compassion and, like so
many of his contemporaries, a fervent Christian, he drew away
from their vigorous certainties. To him power without imagination was itself an evil. "It is the due admixture of romance
and reality that best carries a man through life," he once said.

Henry Lawrence's picture is worth looking at, for he was
among the noblest of all the rich material that went from this
country to the service of India. You see the fine forehead and
the great, brooding eyes, the drawn and patient face. He was
only fifty-one when he died at Lucknow, but he looks an
ageing man. "Grief has made him grey and worn," wrote
Edwardes to Nicholson after his death, "but it became him
like the scars of a battle."

His defeat was the defeat of the best that we could bring
to India. In his humanity and compassion he was more like
the greatest of eastern rulers than the greatest of western
proconsuls. It has been said of him that he left three
memorials, more enduring than the favour of a Viceroy.
There was his grave at Lucknow, which carries out his last
request: "Put on my tomb only this—'Here lies Henry

Lawrence who tried to do his duty. May God have mercy on him'." There were the gardens of the Residency, which he defended and in which he died. And there were the hill-station schools for the children of British soldiers in India, which he somehow found time to found and support in the intervals of his brave laborious life.

Here I must leave what I had begun to say about those of our countrymen who founded and built up the British administration of India. Much was to come after—the Mutiny, the long years that followed, which seemed to look neither back to the past nor forward to a future, and then the efforts to end honourably what these men had honourably begun. I do not touch on this, which is outside my picture. Even with the men I have spoken of I have failed to give any proper taste of their quality or of what they did. It is too diffuse a subject. Nor do these incurious islands care greatly for what is done in their name beyond their sight. These doings will be remembered in a few families, the families which, as Kipling said, served India generation after generation "as dolphins follow in line across the open sea." Plowdens, Trevors, Beadons, Rivett-Carnacs; and I could add a dozen more. But the wind has blown, the hot wind of the Indian plains, and the dust is already drifted over the memory of their achievement. Yet it may be some service to think of them at those times when one falls to wondering whether those who are given power must always use it for selfish ends or forget its purpose in the pride of its possession. When one asks whether there must always be a "governing class" to whom power is to be entrusted, it may help to recall the origins and training of these men. What was their secret? Pride of race? Sense of duty? Sound schooling? All these things were present. And yet the quality that strikes one most is a certain unaffected readiness to be themselves. Goethe noted it in our countrymen. "It lies," he said, "in the courage they have to be that which Nature made them."

LECTURE VI

LECTURE VI

MATTHEW ARNOLD once said that if he merely searched his own consciousness he found that he had no idea of having rights, but only of having duties. He meant to convey that the idea of rights is essentially artificial, something that social habit has conditioned men to look for, but that the deepest part of a man, the real foundation of his being, expresses itself in recognising duties rather than in claiming rights. What would result from Arnold's method of enquiry if the process was applied to ideas such as public opinion, the will of the majority, the will of the people, the will of the nation? It is a question that may help to work towards a clearer understanding of the sanction that lies behind political power, and, on the other hand, to find at what point one can say to authority, "Stop: you can go no further." Somehow, then, one must get an idea of what lies behind the principle of majority rule: because, though democracy is the vaguest of phrases, it is generally regarded as based on the notion that the will of the majority should prevail. What nobody wants and what everybody wants raise no problems. The pinch comes when something is wanted by rather more people than the number who object to it. Now, when that happens, the minority are generally told that they must accept having their wishes overruled, even when they may think, very passionately, that they are in the right and may think (as combatants are apt to do) that the other side are merely being selfish in insisting on having their way. Or it is put more grandly, "Get out, sir: you are thwarting the will of the nation." In the climate of democracy most people, I think, feel abashed at being accused of this and we know that the normal process is that they do accept the majority decision and try to make the best of it. But what is being appealed to when they are told that they are expected to give in? It might be mere force: "We are more than you, we are going to have our way, and we will knock you on the head if you oppose us." There is, I suspect, a stronger element of sheer force at the base of even an advanced democratic society than is usually allowed for by those who give it their praises. But if force were the dominant element, you could only describe the situation as one of tyranny, which must end in explosion and civil war, and the appeal to force is not the real statement of the democratic argument, in this country at any rate. Is there then a process of intellectual conversion that goes on: one man's judgment is as good as another's (which is, after all, the logic of equality), and if 40,000 people want one thing and 20,000 people want another, the 20,000 people must make themselves realise that they are in the wrong? I do not think that will do, not for those who have any strong sense of right and wrong and are not afraid to feel deeply about what they believe in. Besides, I am mixing up what people want with what people think right, and (so far) we have come across no guarantee that the 40,000 people on the other side are even trying to decide impartially what is the best course for everyone. I will try once more. Perhaps the majority's right is based on a rule of give and take? Recurring Parliamentary elections are essential to representative government, and each side may expect in course of time to get its turn of power. This may be so, if there are only two sides. Meantime one side has its innings and knocks up as many runs as it can.

Personally I hate sporting metaphors applied to affairs of State. For one thing they are taken from pursuits in which men show a temper very different from the kind of feeling that prevails when the big political questions are at issue; for another, sports have their own codes and umpires or referees to enforce them. What I am looking for is, what is the code or set of rules that gives validity to a majority decision, apart from the bare fact that it records what the majority's wishes are? And, as I have done before, I will try to get it clearer by seeing what ideas or phrases of this kind have meant to one or two outstanding men of the past.

But, in this case, it must be the recent past, for we are dealing with an idea that is very much of our own day. Nothing ever quite originates in the history of ideas, but the idea that a man must be ruled in everything by the "general will" of the society he lives in can fairly be traced to the genius of Jean-Jacques Rousseau. Even if his theories have been much misunderstood, he remains one of the great formative influences in political thought, one of the men —of whom Karl Marx was another—whose ideas grow to a life larger than the one they live in their creator's work.

Rousseau published the *Social Contract* in 1767. He gave it for its title the popular recipe of the day, but he had no interest in that rather barren business arrangement which John Locke, for instance, describes. Rousseau was going to establish a new basis for man in his relation with the State: something profound and mystical and all-embracing. His theory is extraordinarily hard to disentangle, because so many different Rousseaus keep breaking into the text. There is Rousseau the under-dog, who revenges himself by making fun of all established authority; there is Rousseau the revivalist preacher, who can see in the social bond a "new birth unto righteousness"; and, most elusive of all, there is Rousseau the brilliant journalist, who is fascinated by his own phrases. Indeed they are very good: "Liberty may be gained, but never recovered"; "Wild beasts reign only in the desert"; "Once give money instead of service, and you will soon be in chains"; ". . . to bear with docility the yoke of public happiness"; and the famous opening sentence, "Man is born free and everywhere he is in chains."

Rousseau's book was not designed to strike off those chains. Its purpose was rather to teach that they are self-imposed and to urge the prisoner to find in his servitude a perfect freedom. "Whoso gives himself to all gives himself to none", is another of his sayings. He was a perfectionist, and his mind seems to have revolted from the idea that the authority by which society constrains its members could be force, or contract, or indeed anything but their own free choice. Anything less than that would be inconsistent with human dignity and freedom. So he begins to speak of the act of association which forms a community as an event that substitutes for the person of each of the individuals a new person, a moral and collective body which has unity, self and will. As a member of this new moral body a man should "unceasingly bless the day which freed him for ever from his ancient state". For, "to be subject to appetite is to be a slave, while to obey the laws laid down by society is to be free." In short, Rousseau speaks of a man's conversion into a citizen in very much the same language as St. Paul speaks of a man's conversion to the Christian faith.

The "general will", then, is the will of this new body: an abstract idea. The general will is a tyrant in its rule. "Whoever shall refuse to obey the general will"; he says, "must be constrained by the whole body of his fellow citizens to do so, which is no more than to say that it may be necessary to compel a man to be free." This is the sense in which the people is sovereign, his pregnant phrase; sovereign because the ideal will of the whole community cannot be wrong and is always the master. "The sovereign, by merely existing, is always what it should be." If you called the general will by another set of titles—divine reason, the will of God, our best self, you would, I think, be expressing

Rousseau's idea, though in language that he would have much resented.

This is theory indeed. But when you come to ask how this general will is ascertained in practice, Rousseau eludes your question. The general will turns out to have nothing whatever to do with an ordinary majority decision. It is not even the same thing as the will of all. If all the citizens of a State could be gathered together and if all were to vote on some proposal there would merely be a sum of individual wills and, as these are diverted by party or group interests, a true decision of the common interest, the good of all, would not result. The general will, being an abstraction, remains "constant, pure and unalterable", but in practice it may be thwarted at any time by the wills of real people pursuing their own ends. It is only present, it seems, when everyone votes with no other motive than that of serving the public interest: and as there is no means of being sure whether that has happened or not, one must put aside Rousseau as a guide in practical affairs of statecraft. T. H. Green's criticism of him seems fair to me: "As the will of the people in any other sense than the measure of what the people will tolerate is really unascertainable in the great nations of Europe, the way is prepared for the sophistries of modern political management, for manipulating electoral bodies, for influencing elected bodies and for securing plebiscites."

Now there is a great deal that might be said about the history of these phrases, the general will and the sovereignty of the people. Their true outcome is to exalt the authority of the State over the individual and to support the notion that an individual finds his moral significance in obedience to the State. But I am not now concerned with the triumphs or disasters of that doctrine which, basically, is no ignoble one, because I think that it never had any great effect in this country. It was the words themselves that counted much more than their real meaning. It seems to me that Rousseau's "general will" got crossed with the principles of the Utilitarians, and that it was Bentham, not Rousseau, who broke the older shape of things in England and built up the new structure of majority rule.

What were those principles? I know that I shall not state them adequately, but I will put them this way. First, every man, or at least every sensible, Benthamite sort of man, was the best judge of what was best for himself Therefore the State should interfere as little as possible in his affairs, and its main activity should consist in clearing obstacles from his path and in preventing him from obstructing the like freedom of others. Secondly, one man is as good as another. This is, I think, a vulgarised version of the religious truth that one man is no better than another, since no man knows the measure of the scales of God. Thirdly, the proper end of legislation and, indeed, of human activity is to promote the greatest happiness of the greatest number. Put these three ideas together, and it follows that what a majority of these equally wise, self-regarding persons may happen to want ought to be the law. But drop any one of those ideas overboard and you will find that you are at sea with the rest: cease to believe either that each man is the best judge of his own interest or that it matters greatly whether he is or not, or that men are all equal for the purposes of society, or that.the greatest happiness of the greatest number provides any intelligible test of action and what is left of your faith is not likely to keep society afloat.

Looking back at ideas that are now out of fashion, though, I think, still very influential, one can see that Benthamism was a wonderful destructive force, but less surely valuable as a positive inspiration. "What is the good of you?" is always such a difficult question. It played havoc with privilege that was unjustified and institutions that had lost their purpose, because it challenged them with a test that they could not hope to pass. But, for all that, there must always be privileges

and institutions that can give no adequate answer to a
question so abrupt. Benthamism was produced to fight
existing evils and it ruled badly when it had won its victories
and was left in possession of the field. There is a strong
Puritan flavour in its rejection of State authority and its
elevation of the individual judgment above that authority:
no one, priest or ruler, was to stand between a man and his
God or his duty, or to interpret them to him. The best of the
Utilitarians understood this liberty in the highest sense as the
foundation of a man's moral character. In the same way they
raised the idea of happiness until it came to mean something
that was indistinguishable from virtue. But many people
accepted these convenient principles without being concerned to analyse them at all, and it is not difficult to see
what their general bearing was likely to be. Laws were to
require no other justification than that they expressed what
the majority of people wanted, for selfishness, even though it
was dignified by being called enlightened, was the key to
what would produce the greatest volume of happiness. State
authority was to be suspect and looked down upon, for the
individual judgment was paramount. In fact, the best
service that power could render to the country was to be
feeble.

It seems odd to the spectator that these ideas should have
been reigning at a time when franchise reform was adding
waves of new voters to the electors of Parliament, for they do
not seem well adapted to take the impact of new forces which
might turn out to be revolutionary forces as well. These new
forces might readily share the belief that laws should express
the wants of the majority, while they might forget or ignore
the principle that State power should be weak and reluctant
to interfere. It is here that Walter Bagehot's book on the
English Constitution (I use this adjective) offers such a fascinating commentary on the difference between theory and
practice in British politics.

I deprecate just setting him aside as old-fashioned. His essays were intended to describe the Constitution as it stood in 1865, and, after all, many of us have talked to men who were boys then. He was writing just before Disraeli's Reform Act of 1867, but at a time when extensions of the franchise were not merely in the air but were the subject of definite proposals. He was a very shrewd observer of politics, of a Radical turn, and there is no doubt that his easy, confidential, businesslike way of unravelling constitutional mysteries has had a great influence on readers ever since. The interesting thing is that the landscape that he describes, though its features are the same, seems somehow the landscape of a different country.

Bagehot's picture is, I think, the work of an artist who is both confident and complacent. He has no doubt about the comparative merits of our Constitution—now that it has been tidied up by the nineteenth century—over any other sort of arrangement. The Americans have got hopelessly muddled with their doctrine of the separation of powers and have got a rigid set-up that no business man would tolerate, and the French scream and shout so in debates that they really do not seem fit for Parliamentary institutions at all. But the secret of the English Constitution's merit consists in its nearly complete fusion, through the Cabinet, of the executive and legislative powers. That is one thing; and the other is that the single Chamber of the House of Commons wields absolute power in the country: for, though Bagehot does not actually wish to abolish the monarchy or the House of Lords, indeed he thinks that they both have their uses as being traditional and decorative and so provoking respect from the common people of the country (whose political judgment he does not think much of), still he makes it very plain that he does not consider that they have any right to oppose or get in the way of anything that the House of Commons is really decided about.

A pure theorist of politics might be rather taken aback by all this and might exclaim that what was being described to him was the classic definition of a tyranny. But Bagehot says, No, in fact it works very fairly and reasonably. The clue is that he could not imagine our Constitution without genuine representative government, and therefore he makes the House of Commons the real master of what goes on: not the Cabinet, nor a party organisation, nor the electorate. He speaks of the Cabinet and indeed the Premier as being appointed by the House of Commons; he speaks of the House as seating and unseating Ministries. But then he was writing at a date before the closely organised party had become a dominant factor in politics and his picture of the House of Commons is this: "its various members ought to represent the various special interests, special opinions, special prejudices to be found in the community. There ought to be an advocate for every particular sect, and a vast neutral body of no sect—homogeneous and judicial, like the nation itself." If you can go along with him and regard Parliament as mainly composed of a "vast neutral body of no sect", you have gone a long way towards restoring in another form the separation of powers; because the Cabinet representing the Executive is faced by a block of neutral or middle opinion which it has to satisfy if it is to retain the control of the legislature. That is how Bagehot thought that the system saved itself, in effect by a sort of business-like moderation. It would break down, he says, if parties were made up of warm partisans. "The Body is eager but the atoms are cool. If it were otherwise, parliamentary government would become the worst of governments —a sectarian government." And again: "Our English system . . . . makes party government permanent and possible in the sole way in which it can be so, by making it mild." It seems to me an almost awe-inspiring self-confidence that we should base the success of our Constitution upon a permanent lowness of temperature in our legislators. But

Bagehot is convinced that what the country likes to be ruled by is a body of "sensible men of substantial means", the "heavy sensible class". These, it seems, are supported by public opinion, which is, nowadays, he says, "the opinion of the baldheaded man at the back of the omnibus". Finally, England is a happy instance of the type of "deferential" country, in which the general public takes pleasure in finding that it is ruled by people unlike itself.

But what if people give up their taste for being ruled by heavy sensible men? What if there are not enough bald-headed men on omnibuses to control public opinion? Not that there is anything to cavil at in being bald-headed or on an omnibus : but I do think that there is something deficient in the outlook of a man who can cheerfully describe public opinion in those terms. And what, lastly, if the public ceases to be a deferential public? Not again that there is any better qualification for public affairs than the willingness to defer to the best when we see it : but that is rather a different form of deference. I think that Bagehot's reply to all these questions would be the same : the English Constitution which he knew and praised had passed away.

He may seem to us curiously unaware how much· his existing values might be challenged by anyone who was to drive the idea of equality to its logical conclusion. But, if he was, others were not. The nineteenth century was a century rich in formidable public debaters and equality was to be one of their favourite themes. The opposition carried heavy guns. Acton, Newman, Froude, Carlyle, Ruskin, Matthew Arnold, Huxley, Fitzjames Stephen, Sumner Maine : starting from what were often quite different premises they joined to attack the whole principle of equality. Not political equality, the sharing of equal political rights, which most of them treated as unimportant in itself, but the idea of individual equality, one man's judgment as good as another's, which is the true foundation of a majority's tyranny. For, once government by privilege was seen to be a defeated system, men turned to the question whether representative systems and self-government were by themselves any necessary protection against this newer form of despotism. Even John Stuart Mill recognised this. "The will of the people . . . " he says in his essay *On Liberty*, " practically means the will of the most numerous or the most active part of the people : the majority or those who succeed in making themselves accepted as the majority : the people, consequently, may desire to oppress a part of their number, and precautions are as much needed against this as against any other abuse of power." Mill stands apart from the others as the inheritor of the tradition of the Utilitarians, and he stands apart from the other Utilitarians as much the most persuasive and gracious expounder of their doctrines. So persuasive that it is sometimes said that he transformed them into something else. He at any rate was firm in the belief that government by consent, given a true representative system, was the noblest form of government that men could live under. But his book on *Representative Government*, published in 1861, makes rather sad reading, for one sees how many were the qualifications and how stern the requirements that he laid down for its success. Almost he seems at times to say with Rousseau, "Were there such a thing as a nation of Gods it would be a democracy. So perfect a form of government is not suited to mere men."

Mill's sovereign remedy for the ills that attend democracy is Proportional Representation, for he thought that this was the only device that would ensure minorities the right to be heard: and with Mill—a man of whom John Morley said, "Respect for him became an element of men's own self-respect"—the right to have a grievance heard was the right to have a grievance redressed. He believed ardently in the justice of Proportional Representation, a scheme by which like-minded voters of a sufficient number, could, as it were, form their own constituency. Such a scheme has never been operated in this country, though we have certainly not heard the last of it. At least it is calculated to get a minority group to Westminster instead of leaving it in the constituencies, scattered and unrepresented. Like many of his contemporaries Mill was uneasy when he thought what might happen to Parliamentary institutions under the onrush of new voters. Their fears seem exaggerated when one looks back, but they were, after all, facing an electorate in which there existed no general system of education at all. He was perhaps less like his contemporaries in having the courage to propose statutory qualifications for voters: they should have some educational acquirement, they should bear some share of taxation and not be in receipt of poor relief, there should be plurality of votes for mental superiority, but not for property. Years afterwards Mill wrote of his advocacy of such measures: "As far as I have been able to observe, it has found favour with nobody: all who desire any sort of inequality in the electoral vote desiring it in favour of property and not of intelligence or knowledge."

Two things sustained him among all his misgivings for the future of what he felt ought to be, and yet might so well not be, the highest form of government. One was his belief in the value of free discussion, the other his belief in liberty. It seems cheap to say now that he much overestimated the importance of the first and that he attributed to men more readiness than they possess to let their actions be governed by rational discussion. But I cannot help thinking that he did greatly exaggerate the rational element in discussion. When I work through Mills's books and the counterblast of his critic, Fitzjames Stephen, *Liberty, Equality, Fraternity*, I am left at the end with the feeling that both side's arguments are so close, so logical, so merciless in their terms that somehow real life has been squeezed out in the process. But when Mill stops arguing and explains his general conception of liberty, his words are memorable. To him it was an absolute value. If men could bring his passion to their thought of it, if they could feel his reverence in their respect for it, here indeed would be the answer to all aggressions of governments and powers. I know that his definition is not the whole truth, that it can be criticised as inadequate, because it is a negative, and that the very terms in which he defines it can be turned upon themselves: but here is something at least which belongs to the permanent structure of English thought, words which should be scrubbed into the minds of all the petty tyrants of our fields. Liberty of conscience, thought and opinion; of expression, taste or pursuit; of association and combination. He lists them all, and then, "No society in which these liberties are not, on the whole, respected is free, whatever may be its form of government; and none is completely free in which they do not exist absolute and unqualified. The only freedom which deserves the name is that of pursuing our own good in our own way, so long as we do not deprive others of theirs or impede their efforts to obtain it. Each is the proper guardian of his own health, whether bodily or mental or spiritual. Mankind are greater gainers by suffering each other to live as seems good to themselves than by compelling each to live as seems good to the rest."

LECTURE VII

LECTURE VII

THERE comes a time, after one has been thinking about
the nature of power, when power seems to take on a life
and character of its own. It separates itself from the men who
use it or are used by it and the study of its laws becomes an
independent scientific enquiry. De Tocqueville taught his
readers to see a tragic force at work in history, which drives
men to build up the very institutions that are to make slaves
of them. When I read M. de Jouvenel's recent remarkable
study *Du Pouvoir* I find that he too speaks of power as if it
were some terrible and remorseless god with laws that deter-
mine both the nature of his own being and the fate of men
who fall into his hand. Not because men worship power itself.
Some do; there is a dynamism in the mere exercise of power
that, to one way of thinking, supplies its whole meaning. On
that view power justifies itself by being power. But the mor-
bid pathology of human ambition is another study: what I
am thinking of is the picture of power presented to us as
something inherently greedy, jealous and corrupting. History
gives a rich enough background for this central figure.

Yet power is not a thing in itself. Take away the abstract
idea and there remains nothing but the conduct of men,
human beings, who occupy in their turn the seats of authority.
It does not seem to me that there is only one possible
attitude towards authority or one inevitable set of rules that
govern its exercise. Attitudes change with the social conditions which surround authority and, as we have seen, men in
their turn exalt and denigrate power under the impulse of
their general attitude towards life itself. You can see it your
own way, so long as you know what that way is. It reminds

99

me of an old saying: " 'Take what you want', said God; 'take it, and pay for it.' "

We have seen too that men try to confine power within bounds, bounds drawn sometimes from religious ideas, sometimes from philosophical ideas. Sometimes bounds are imposed by actual conditions, not by ideas at all. But it is ideas rather than situations that I have been seeking to talk about. Ideas seem to me so much more important. They have a life of their own, which does not depend on their being realised in practice, which is independent even of their being misapplied or perverted. They are therefore immortal or, rather, endlessly reborn.

One attitude is to be afraid of power. That is not a poor or cowardly attitude in face of the reckless use that men have made of their authority over other men. But if mistrust is the dominant note, then it may be best expressed by such constitutional devices as those of the American Constitution. Power is placed under restraint; it is deliberately shared out so that it cannot all be grasped in the same hand. A constitution, plainly, is not an elemental force. In itself it is a piece of parchment or, if you will, a contract between the living people who made it. The Constitution is effective to maintain its controls in the United States because generations of people who have belonged to those States have continued to believe that on the whole such controls are wise and desirable. There is there a respect for the Constitution and a general understanding of its import that mean a good deal. The men who made it did very deliberately intend to secure that the affairs of the Union should not be at the mercy of any easy doctrines about the will of the people; they were not dazzled by the moral claims of majorities to have their way. Yet under the shadow of this Constitution a vast immigration took place and a great democracy has grown up, and, though America had much else to offer to those "huddled masses yearning to breathe free" whose welcome is inscribed on the Statue of Liberty in New York harbour, the protection of its Constitution, individual right above the lawmaking power of your fellow citizens, was one of the things that it had to give. So you may see in the United States a genuine belief in the virtue and sovereignty of what Mr. Henry Wallace has called "the common man" side by side with a respected tradition that no man or group of men is virtuous enough to hold the privilege of power unchecked.

What, now, is the true attitude towards power in this country? For, however widely one may range to catch an idea here or an aspect there, one comes home in the end to one's own affairs. We have not got any written Constitution on which there can be, as it were, inscribed a national point of view. That means that attitudes can change quicker, and can change too without it being easy to observe the alteration. Some things have gone so completely that their main use is to remind us how different their shape has been. The feudal system, privileged corporations, privileged classes, aristocratic influence: power as ruled by universal law, power as a duty in this world to be answered for in the next, power as the job of an agent under a contract. These ideas are part of history, but they do not rule any more. On the other hand, we have not outgrown the tradition that there are a citizen's rights standing between him and despotic power; certainly they exist, and exist by a very ancient tenure which brave men have had to vindicate in the past. Those rights are said to have this peculiarity, that they have been, in the main, won in the courts of law; they have been upheld by judges as rights which exist by the immemorial custom of the country under the common law and they have not been created therefore by any deliberate act of constitution-making. No doubt that could be said quite truly when it was said by Professor Dicey towards the end of the last century. But there are qualifications upon what he said that

make it less important than it may seem. Firstly, these great
victories in the law courts were won against the power of the
Crown, the executive, upon whom the common law, the
ancient custom, always did impose limits. There was no
English tradition that gave an arbitrary power to the King or
his servants. But such victories could never be won against
the force of anything sanctioned by an Act of Parliament,
because that is final law in our courts and every judge must
give effect to it. Now that the executive and the law-making
power are to all intents and purposes the same, because both
powers have fallen into the same hands, those of the ruling
political party, these victories do not stand for the same kind
of security as in the past. An Act of Parliament can reverse
them at any moment. It always could, and I am not saying
at all that any particular Parliament or indeed any Parliament
is likely to be indifferent to maintaining these long-established
traditions; but it is only sensible to see that with what is,
practically, single-chamber Government and with executive
and legislative combined, the security of what used to be
called constitutional rights is a frail thing. Secondly, many
rights that one can only call constitutional are to-day
the product of Acts of Parliament and nothing else. For
instance, all the bundle of rights that depend on National
Insurance. They seem, I suppose, just as much fundamental to our scheme of society as, say, freedom from
arbitrary arrest or the right of free assembly, which are two
rights, always spoken of as constitutional, that originate in
the common law. Yet rights given by Parliament, just like
rights originating in the common law, can be added to,
altered or taken away by Parliament. Their title to be called
fundamental is only a courtesy title. When I see our system
praised as embodying the "rule of law", I cannot help
recalling Alexander Hamilton's saying: "It is one thing to be
subordinate to the laws and another to be dependent on the
legislative body."

What does the "rule of law" mean? Any attempt to analyse it will show how elusive our ideas of power can turn out to be. Rule of law may mean one thing in terms of international law and another thing at home. No doubt it means something different to an American from what it does to an Englishman, but Americans and British are both fond of using the phrase as descriptive of a common element in their civilisation. It cannot just mean a general readiness to abide by the law. I do not know that either country is outstanding in that respect, and anyway you could find as great a readiness in any country that had a strong and effective force of government. Professor Dicey, who is looked to as the classic exponent of what is involved in the modern idea of a rule of law, laid down that it had three features: the executive had no arbitrary powers over the individual, no powers that had not been sanctioned either by Parliament or by the common law, every one is subject to the ordinary law of the realm and can have his rights determined in the ordinary courts; and thirdly, the main principles of the Constitution, such as the right of personal liberty or of public meeting, have been set up on the foundation of the old common law and not as things derived from any general constitutional theory. Well, of course, freedom from arbitrary arrest and the right to have your personal affairs decided by ordinary law and in the ordinary courts, even when the power of the State is on the other side, do represent very valuable curbs on executive power. But then Dicey goes on to say about "Administrative Law": "The notion which lies at the bottom of the 'administrative law' known to foreign countries is that affairs or disputes in which the government or its servants are concerned are beyond the sphere of the civil courts, and must be dealt with by special and more or less official bodies. This idea is utterly unknown to the law of England and indeed is fundamentally inconsistent with our traditional customs." But, if administrative law and the rule of law are fundamentally inconsistent things, we have certainly said goodbye to an essential element in the rule of law by now, because although we do not have Courts of High Commission or Star Chambers to-day, Parliament has for a good many years been creating all sorts of "special and more or less official bodies"—commissioners, arbitrators, referees and what not—which are charged with deciding this or that question arising under the provision of an Act of Parliament and which do in fact dispose of the affairs of individual citizens without their having a chance of reaching an ordinary court of law. I do not at all say that this is wrong, although obviously it can be abused, nor do I see how it could have been avoided under the sort of administration that modern society requires. Indeed, I can see a lot of truth in the view that a conflict between the individual and the public administration is different in kind from a conflict between one individual and another and may require a different approach. But that is beside what I am talking about. All that I have been saying leads me to think that under our system ideas and attitudes are unusually fluid, at any rate towards this sort of subject, and that great words such as constitutional rights, liberty and the rule of law seem to change their meaning even while one looks at them.

There is one remedy for all this vexation, though I do not myself recommend it. It is to assume that everything will somehow go all right with this country just because it is this country, which has always got along by ignoring what wise people have said or what other peoples have done. In fact it is to be a Walter Bagehot, and to assume that somehow there will always be a "due succession of fit persons", bald-headed men on the backs of omnibuses or whatever may be the current equivalent, to make sure that things are done in a "heavy, sensible way." But surely this is to assume a very special covenant with destiny. The British character is one of our great State institutions, perhaps the greatest, but it is an illusion to suppose that moderation and tolerance must always be among its conspicuous virtues. It is quite possible that they were the hall-mark of a particular class and of economic conditions that were on the whole continuously improving. There has been no lack of zealots and fanatics in the history of the British Isles and the strain is not likely to die out with changing economic conditions, changing values and with what is, I believe, a very general feeling that toleration is, after all, only a qualified form of virtue.

Perhaps I am wrong in thinking that that feeling spreads. Speaking of these abstractions I remember de Tocqueville's words at the outbreak of the French Revolution of 1848, "We entrusted ourselves to the Future, an enlightened and impartial judge, if you please, but one who sits alas! always too late." "Nous nous confiames à l'avenir juge éclairé et intègre, mais qui arrive hélas! toujours trop tard." But does liberty or freedom mean the same in 1951 as it meant, say, in the famous passage of John Stuart Mill that I read last time? "The only freedom which deserves the name is that of pursuing our own good in our own way, so long as we do not deprive others of theirs or impede their efforts to obtain it." That is, essentially, an assertion that the individual has an absolute right to be left alone wherever his conduct does not interfere with a like liberty in others. Changing views in society will always make it uncertain what is the extent of that sphere in which a man's conduct does not injure others, but the force of Mill's argument lies in the belief that all moral progress, the whole development of the best in a man, depends on his being free to make his own independent choice. To coerce him, to require him to conform, even to lead him, unless with his spontaneous intellectual approbation, was to do him wrong because it involved depriving him of his most important opportunities. "Where not the person's own character", he says, "but the traditions and customs of other people, are the rule of conduct, there is wanting one of the principal ingredients of human happiness and quite the chief ingredient of individual and social progress." This austere doctrine of individual responsibility had in it much of our own history: the Puritan, with his insistence on man's direct relation with his God; the Dissenter, to whom State authority stood for galling oppression and interference; the merchant and industrialist, to whom in the past government had so often meant the same thing as obstruction.

I do not know the final moral basis of Mill's liberty. There is deep in most men a feeling that virtue attained after temptation and struggle is of a higher order than virtue that comes without effort: that, as Francis Thomspon wrote, "the harvest waves richest over the battlefields of the soul". Yet it does not seem right to value the way to the result more than the result itself; to prize, so to say, the athletic type of sainthood more than the natural, flower-like quality that it sometimes shows. The truth is, I think, that Mill's idea of liberty represents one kind but not the only kind, nor necessarily the highest kind, of freedom. When President Roosevelt spoke of the "Four Freedoms" some years ago, many people thought that he was offering a fine summary of the kind of liberties that a democratic people could cherish as the basis of their society. Yet one of these was styled "freedom from want" and another "freedom from fear". Neither of them is freedom in the older sense, the right of an individual not to be interfered with by the power of society; on the contrary they are the reverse, they are claims of the individual to be dependent upon society. There is nothing in itself derogatory in the notion of dependence, the "unbought grace of life". There is dependence in the highest form of human relationships, as there is in the clinging of the parasite. But one may perhaps infer that liberty looked upon as the right to find and to try to realise the best that is in oneself is not something to which power is necessarily hostile: more, such liberty may even need the active intervention of authority to make it possible. It has been part of the cant of English life for so long to speak of power as an evil thing, an intoxicating thing, a corrupting thing. I call it cant because all experience shows that the British are singularly fitted to the exercise of authority and by no means go mad or become ruthless tyrants when entrusted with great responsibilities. But give a dog a bad name and you give him a licence to behave badly.

There is a tradition of life in these islands that both ennobles and restrains authority. Only it lives in the spirit, and has no special form to express it. I can use a last word to explain what I mean if I take the names of three great writers of the nineteenth century, Ruskin, Carlyle and Matthew Arnold. The world of their own day admired them and passed them by. Now, a hundred years later, it is easier to see how true their instinct was. None of the three was primarily a political writer; but each of them came to find himself defending the spiritual value of authority. Ruskin, starting from a study of aesthetics, found something intolerable in an economic and social system in which no man acknowledged any guide but that of his own wit and taste. But it was always possible to remember that he was, after all, an art critic and to treat his economics and his social philosophy as a little off his beat. Carlyle, too, was primarily a historian, and, it must be said, *Heroes and Hero Worship* and *Past and Present* are heavy reading. The great over-charged sentences come storming up and break in deluge on your head. One gets tired of being told of each hero in turn that he was a noble-hearted, sincere man who saw direct into the burning heart of things. One gets wistful at this sort of windy advice: "Find in any country the Ablest Man that exists there; raise him to the supreme place and loyally reverence him: you have a perfect government for that country: no ballot box, parliamentary eloquence, voting, constitution building

or other machinery whatever can improve it. It is the perfect
State: the ideal country."

Tell us something practical, one says. But when the storm
and wind are over, the majesty of Carlyle, the secret of his
influence, is this, that he does bring home that the best in us
wants to be ruled by the best that others can reveal to us.
That best is the real common wealth. For him a great man
stands for great things and, as he says, it needs heroes to
follow a hero. "Liberty?" he says, "the true Liberty of a
man you would say consisted in his finding out, or being
forced to find out the right path, and to walk thereon. To
learn, or to be taught, that work he actually was able for; and
then by permission, persuasion and even compulsion, to set
about doing of the same. That is his true blessedness, honour,
liberty and maximum of well being: if liberty be not that I
for one have small care about liberty. . . . That I have been
called by all Newspapers a freeman will avail me little if my
pilgrimage have ended in death and wreck. . . . Liberty
requires new definitions."

It is a doctrine that can easily be abused, but I do not
know that he is saying anything of liberty that had not already
been said by Plato and St. Paul.

I do not know how widely Matthew Arnold's *Culture and
Anarchy* is read nowadays. It must be one of the most
brilliant and, beside that, one of the most perceptive books
of the nineteenth century. Arnold reflected such different
aspects of thought; in *Culture and Anarchy* there is none of
the sad uncertainties of his poetry, "the unplumbed, salt,
estranging sea" and the "ignorant armies" that "clash by
night". Here he is up in arms. He had been stung by criticisms of himself as being tepid and detached in the cause
of human welfare because he had shown no enthusiasm for
various Liberal Party measures of the hour: and he replies
with the delicate and unpitying precision of an artist who has
been annoyed. His theme is simple. Acts of Parliament, like

other actions, are not good or bad just because they are
vigorously advocated or because a lot of well-meaning people
energetically desire them. Such things can only be judged by
bringing to bear upon them the best that has been thought or
said in the past about the nature and purpose of human life
and testing their value in the light that will thus play upon
them. This is not a plea for culture; it is a plea for the use of
culture in the direction of public affairs. Culture is a word
that makes some people in this country reach for their guns—
like Marshal Goering; but I do not see how a country that is
worth living in can get on without a reverence for it. It is the
only thing that can harmonise the individual interests,
passions and desires that tear a community apart. It is a
bigger thing than tolerance, because it does not merely stand
by; but, like tolerance, it is, says Arnold, "the eternal
opponent of the two things which are the signal marks of
Jacobinism—its fierceness and its addiction to an abstract
system." This is how he builds up his case: "by our everyday
selves, however, we are separate, personal, at war; we are
only safe from one another's tyranny when no one has any
power; and this safety in its turn cannot save us from
anarchy." Anarchy, to him, represents not only no power of
government, but no authority outside our own will and
judgment. There is, he says, "a kind of philosophical theory
widely spread among us to the effect that there is no such
thing at all as a best self and a right reason having claim to
paramount authority or, at any rate, no such thing ascertain-
able and capable of being made use of; and that there is
nothing but an infinite number of ideas, works of our ordinary
selves . . . which are doomed either to an irreconcilable
conflict, or else to a perpetual give and take; and that wisdom
consists in choosing the give and take rather than the conflict
and in sticking to our choice with patience and good humour."

This he calls a "peculiarly British form of atheism", as
indeed it is, for it denies the existence of any supreme value.

And he finds a "peculiarly British form of Quietism" in an alternative theory that everything ought to be, as it were, allowed its fling, in the hope that the common reason of society will prevent anything going altogether too far. This attitude, he says, shows a devout, but excessive, reliance on an over-ruling Providence.

Culture, to Arnold, does necessarily imply a standard of authority outside ourselves, for it is the standard of all wise and beautiful things. Yet there is a self in us that draws to that standard and is ruled by it, and this best self we share with others. "We want an authority", he says, "and we find nothing but jealous classes, checks and a deadlock; culture suggests the idea of the State. We find no basis for a firm State power in our ordinary selves; culture suggests one to us in our best self." The State is an organ of our collective best self or our national right reason; and he quotes, to be, as it were, the motto of all authority and all power, the words of Bishop Wilson, "Firstly, never go against the best light you have; secondly, take care that your light be not darkness."

And there I leave it, for I know no better guide. Take care that your light be not darkness. Think it possible, as Cromwell said, that you be mistaken. That is the humane man's warning to all zealotry, all fanaticism. But, after the warning, power, authority, dominion are still with us, they correspond to something that belongs to a man's inmost self, and men do themselves no service by thinking or speaking of them as evil things. Power is good or evil according to the vision that it serves: not the vision of governors alone, nor the vision of governed alone, but a vision that is somehow common to them both, though not discerned with equal range of sight. And vision, as I see it, is not the right to dream or the gift of prophecy, but, more humbly, the best light that we have.

DATE DUE

McLEAN, TORONTO FORM #38-297